Selected Poems and Prose of John Davidson

Selected Poems and Prose of John Davidson

EDITED BY

JOHN SLOAN

CLARENDON PRESS · OXFORD

1995

Oxford University Press, Walton Street, Oxford OX2 6DP
Oxford New York
Athens Auckland Bangkok Bombay
Calcutta Cape Town Dar es Salaam Delhi
Florence Hong Kong Istanbul Karachi
Kuala Lumpur Madras Madrid Melbourne
Mexico City Nairobi Paris Singapore
Taipei Tokyo Toronto
and associated companies in
Berlin Ibadan

Oxford is a trade mark of Oxford University Press

Published in the United States
by Oxford University Press Inc., New York

British Library Cataloguing in Publication Data
Data available

Library of Congress Cataloging in Publication Data
Davidson, John, 1857–1909.
[Selections. 1995]
John Davidson: selected poems and prose/[edited by] John Sloan.
1. Scotland—Poetry. 2. England—Poetry. 3. Davidson, John, 1857–1909—Correspondence. 4. Poets, Scottish—19th century—Correspondence. I. Sloan, John, 1948– . II. Title. III. Title: Selected poems and prose.
PR4525.D5A6 1995 821′.8—dc20 95–1323
ISBN 0–19–818335–6

1 3 5 7 9 10 8 6 4 2

Typeset by Best-set Typesetter Ltd., Hong Kong
Printed in Great Britain
on acid-free paper by
Bookcraft Ltd,
Midsomer Norton, Avon

Contents

PROSE

LETTERS

Introduction

JOHN DAVIDSON has always been a difficult poet to place. Is he Scottish or English? A poet of the Decadence or of the counter-Decadence? Is he a minor lyricist of the 1890s, or does the ambitious poetry of his later years place him among the major poets? Are his scientific theories the enemy of poetry? Whatever the answers, John Davidson's work has mattered to a remarkable number of people. In 1957, both T. S. Eliot and Hugh MacDiarmid warmly admitted their debt to him on the centenary of his birth. Eliot singled out Davidson's 'Thirty Bob a Week' as the poem which prepared him 'for initiation into the work of some of the French symbolists, such as Laforgue'.[1] For MacDiarmid, Davidson's importance lay in his interest in scientific material and in urban experience, as well as in his experiments in form and language.[2] Today Davidson is acknowledged by many to be the best Scottish poet between Robert Burns and MacDiarmid—Robert Crawford places him in the tradition of bicultural 'British' writers such as Walter Scott (1771–1832) and Thomas Carlyle (1795–1881) whose work questions the Anglocentricity of 'English' literature[3]—while more generally he is admired as an early modern, whose fascination with urban experience and the new technologies of the modern world supplied a precedent for the Modernist movement.

Given the identification of Modernism as international and cosmopolitan, John Davidson would seem an unlikely candidate for the role of 'first of the moderns'. Born at Barrhead, Renfrewshire in 1857, Davidson was brought up in the Clydeside port of Greenock, just over twenty miles from Glasgow. His father, Alexander Davidson, was a minister of the secessionist Evangelical Union which rejected the Calvinist idea of the Elect for a liberal theology based on salvation for all men.

[1] Quoted in 'Introduction', *John Davidson: A Selection of his Poems*, ed. Maurice Lindsay (London, 1961), 9; originally in Maurice Lindsay, 'John Davidson: The Man Forbid', *Saltire Review*, 4 (1957), 57.

[2] 'John Davidson: Influences and Influence', in *John Davidson: A Selection*, ed. Lindsay, 47–54.

[3] Robert Crawford, *Devolving English Literature* (Oxford, 1992).

Although Davidson was to decry the 'Philistinism' and 'murky atmosphere of Greenock' in which he had been brought up,[4] his background proved extremely valuable to him as a poet. The hero of his powerful autobiographical poem, 'A Ballad in Blank Verse' (1894), lives in 'the North':

> . . . where Old and New
> Welter upon the border of the world,
> And savage creeds can kill.
>
> (ll. 356–8)[5]

In Davidson's writings 'the North' indicates a double identity. On the one hand it means 'Scottishness'. Like many Scotsmen, he had a romantic interest in the Scottish War of Independence, evident in his early chronicle-play *Bruce*, and in the tragedy of the Stuart kings. But for Davidson, 'the North' also meant 'North Britain'. In an interview in 1901 he asserted that the Scottish War of Independence was the most important event in the history of the British Empire 'for if the English had conquered the Scotch, there would have been no British Empire'.[6] What seems on the face of it a cocky display of Scottish independence also expresses a characteristic Scottish pride in the contribution of the Scots to the larger sense of 'Britishness'. Greenock itself embraced both these identities—the romantic and the modern, Scottishness and Britishness—in a symbolic way. The town was proud of its monument to Burns's Highland Mary, who was buried in the Old West Kirk, while it named its streets and civic buildings after its most famous native son, James Watt, the inventor of the steam-engine. While Davidson was growing up, Greenock was an important seaport of the British Empire, and a centre for the foreign missions.

Davidson's literary outlook reflected this doubleness from very early on. His reading as a child included Walter Scott along with John Bunyan and Charles Kingsley, and at 12 he immersed himself with equal enthusiasm in Shakespeare's sonnets and

[4] Letter to A. C. Swinburne, 28 Mar. 1878, in Cecil Y. Lang (ed.), *The Swinburne Letters*, iv (New Haven, Conn., 1960), 47–8.

[5] *Ballads and Songs* (London, 1894), 29–30.

[6] 'About Myself', *Candid Friend*, (1901), 177–8.

Carlyle's *Sartor Resartus* (1834). But it was Scott and Carlyle who were to be decisive in shaping his literary manner. From Carlyle he developed a humorous, fantastical turn of mind. This is evident in his first published work, the novel *The North Wall* (1885; reissued in 1891 as *A Practical Novelist*)—in which literature and life become confused—and in his later fictional collaborations with C. J. Wills, where the action is halted by humorous commentary on such subjects as Scots words or the process of writing. From Scott, he formed a lifelong attachment to the ballad form, in which oral traditions and the sophistications of metropolitan culture meet, as they were again to do in Modernism. His first poem, written as a twelve-year-old, was a heroic ballad on 'The Defeat of the Moors by Ramiro, King of Spain'. Crawford's definition of the eclectic, anthropological tendencies in both Scott and Carlyle as 'proto-Modernist' seems especially relevant in the context of Davidson's indebtedness to both writers.[7]

By the age of 19, when he completed an apprenticeship as a pupil-teacher and left Greenock for Edinburgh University, Davidson was also an enthusiastic reader of translations—Goethe, presumably on account of Carlyle—and of Spenser's *Faerie Queen*, Milton's *Comus*, and John Lyly's prose romance, *Euphues*. In 1878, after an abortive term at Edinburgh University, he returned to teaching in Glasgow, where he came under the influence of John Nichol, who was then Professor of English Literature at Glasgow University. There may be some paradox in the designation of a chair of 'English' literature at one of Scotland's oldest universities, but Nichol's literary interests were much broader than the term would suggest and included Scottish as well as American and Continental writers. In Nichol's circle Davidson developed an enthusiasm for the so-called 'Spasmodic' school of Scottish poets, among them Alexander Smith, author of *A Life Drama* (1853) and *City Poems* (1857), who appears to have influenced Davidson's Spasmodic drama *Smith: A Tragedy*, which he dedicated to Nichol. Burns too was admired. Among the close friends he made in Nichol's circle was a young Burns scholar and student of Scottish dialect, John George Dow, later Professor of Literature at the state

[7] Crawford, *Devolving English Literature*.

universities of Vermillion, South Dakota, and Madison. Davidson's own attitude to Burns was complex. He shared Burns's scorn for hypocrisy and superstition—his good-humoured satire on the Calvinist doctrine of hell in 'The Rev. Habakkuk McGruther, of Cape Wrath' is in the Burnsian manner—but he generally deplored Burnsian imitation and the artificial use of 'Braid Scots'.

The speaker of 'Ayrshire Jock', one of his earliest monologues, ridicules the 'mongrel Scotch' of those who 'imitate the lad of Kyle'. Drinking alone in his Glasgow garret, Aryshire Jock presents himself as a realist who writes in the English tradition for an educated readership. Yet the ironies of his situation are not lost on himself or the reader, as he tries to blank out his happy memories of a rural childhood and his present loneliness as a struggling city poet. The stress on the harshness of reality; the combination of high and low in the serio-comic vernacular address: these are derived from the traditions of Scottish dramatic utterance. English poetry also has its dramatic monologue—interestingly it was Davidson who was summoned hurriedly by the *Glasgow Herald* newspaper in 1889 to write a leader when Robert Browning died in Venice—but the acting-out of the feelings of others in their more spontaneous, living speech occurs more often in Scottish poetry. One also finds this in Davidson's early songs. His 'Piper, Play!' is a communal song which expresses the harsh reality of factory life. His poetic model was Thomas Hood's 'The Song of the Shirt', composed about 1843.

Davidson also adapted the dramatic monologue to contemporary subject-matter in his sequence of 'In a Music-Hall' poems, which he wrote while working as a clerk in Glasgow in 1884. 'Selene Eden', the fifth speaker in the sequence, is an erotic-dance artiste, who reveals the secrets of her trade. Like many writers and artists of the day, Davidson was fascinated by the music-hall, which in the late-Victorian age had become a theatrical compendium of the popular and the affectedly high-brow. In an astute response to these music-hall poems when they came out in London in 1891, W. B. Yeats linked Davidson and Arthur Symons as poets who looked for 'new subject matter, new emotions' in 'the common pleasures of common men', and in the 'rough accidents of life'.[8] Davidson seemed to have Yeats's review still in mind over two years later when he dismissed Symons's obsession with prostitutes as 'a common mood of common men' in his reader's report on Symons's *London Nights* (1895) for his publisher, John Lane.[9] Clearly he resented Yeats's comparison. One can understand why. Both poets share a sense of the falsely gay, of life being like a music-hall, but Symons is a voyeur of the boulevard and theatre, the aesthete in search of Baudelairean sensation and the living symbol of the self-obsessed artist. Davidson, in contrast, aims for a dramatic sympathy with his music-hall artistes through the ironic re-creation of their surface-tricks of speech and gesture.

'Thirty Bob a Week', in which a London clerk curses and questions the miseries of his situation, is Davidson's most successful transformation of the music-hall idiom into serious verse. Readers have sometimes been puzzled by T. S. Eliot's high claims for the poem, which seems on the face of it to achieve little more than Kipling's *Barrack-Room Ballads* (1892). But there is more to the poem than its Kiplingesque exploitation of lower-class speech. In 'Thirty Bob a Week', the disgruntled, socially insecure clerk combines colloquial and cultured language in a way that conveys his sense of inner division and feelings of a double life. In this, and in his desire to link his existence to a more primitive law of nature, Davidson's clerk anticipates Eliot's 'J. Alfred Prufrock'.

Davidson's poetic range was unquestionably broadened by his move to London with his wife and two small boys when he was 32. In London he was exposed to the new literary and artistic ideas that circulated in Fleet Street, where he worked, among the Rhymers, who met at the Cheshire Cheese on Friday nights to read their verses, and in the Bohemian circles that gathered at William Sharp's house in Hampstead and Robert Sherard's Charles Street rooms, where Oscar Wilde was a frequent visitor. His public face in those early London days was that of the outspoken, rough-mannered Scotsman. This is how Yeats and the Rhymers remembered him, and how he carica-

[8] W. B. Yeats, 'The Rhymers' Club', *Boston Pilot* (23 Apr. 1892); repr. in *Letters to the New Island*, ed. Horace Reynolds (Cambridge, Mass., 1934).

[9] MS. Walpole d. 17, not dated, Bodleian Library, Oxford.

tured himself in the figure of Rorison, the excitable Scotsman in *Earl Lavender.* It was a cultural stance of directness and impatience with metropolitan refinement that he brought to his poetry.

His first poetic success came with the publication of his first series of *Fleet Street Eclogues* in 1893. His original idea had been to write a teacher's calendar based on Spenser's *Shepherd's Calendar* (1579). The change of scene to Fleet Street was a fortunate one, allowing greater contrast between town and country experience, reality and imagination, the simple language of pastoral and the mass telecommunications of modern metropolitan life. Although his model was Spenser, the inspiration for the Eclogues came from Chambers's *Book of Days* (1863–4), which takes its epigraph for each month from Spenser. Like Scott and Carlyle, Davidson was a gatherer of odd facts, a literary anthropologist and *bricoleur,* preferring to go for inspiration to dictionaries and encyclopaedias than to the works of other poets, although he had no scruple in borrowing from other writers. The spirit of the Eclogues is antiquarian: traditional saints' days, folk legends, and country customs are assembled in an effort to achieve a new unity and meaningfulness in a world where such traditions are only a memory.

The absence evoked throughout the Eclogues is the kingdom of God. Davidson's journalists and pressmen may carry 'Eden in their heart' ('Good Friday'), but their world is godless rather than fallen—the Church 'a lifeboat warped and sunk' ('St Swithin's Day'). In an early essay, T. S. Eliot described Scotland as a 'nation which had been ruined by religion', and which 'took religion more seriously than the English'.[10] But arguably, it was the intensity of Davidson's Scottish Presbyterian upbringing and his quarrel with it that favourably positioned him to become a distinctively modern voice in the London of the 1890s. He composed the first Eclogues in one of his father's old theological notebooks, after removing some pages of notes a few months after Alexander Davidson's death in December 1891. Underlying the diverse voices of the Eclogues is his sense of separation from his father's faith. In contrast to a father who

[10] T. S. Eliot, 'Byron', in Bonamy Dobrée ed., *From Anne to Victoria: Essays by Various Hands* (London, 1937), 603.

'believed every word he spoke',[11] he found himself driven by irony and self-division. His pressmen and would-be poets find their momentary consolations in dewy boyhood memories, in recollections of the country, in holiday songs and rituals, in the journalists' prayer that concludes 'St Swithin's Day', but these have a ghostly fictive quality amid the rumble and roar of the modern metropolis. This hallucinatory element becomes stronger in Davidson's second series of *Fleet Street Eclogues*, published in 1896, where the gulf between the dungeon city and the Edens of the mind seems even greater. In [Confessions of a Haunted Mind], from 'Lammas', Ninian's moments of visionary ecstasy are haunted by neurosis and fears of insanity.

In 'Christmas Eve'—restored here to its original form—'A Ballad of Hell' provides an imaginative triumph over the guilty dread of sin and 'Other World'. The dramatic context gives the recitation of the ballad a communal meaning beyond the artificial 'museum life' that threatens the ballad form. When Davidson encouraged the publication of his ballads as a group in the 1890s, including 'A Ballad of Hell', he had already discovered a receptive circle of readers to whom they appealed directly. This is particularly true of his 'A Ballad of a Nun', which was immensely popular when it first appeared in the *Yellow Book* in October 1894. While 'Thirty Bob a Week' has always had admirers, 'A Ballad of a Nun' has not stood the test of time so well. The visual and auditory detail is still beautiful, but the tale of the young nun, a portress, who escapes from the convent to satisfy her sexual longings, only to discover that the Virgin Mary has taken her place as keeper of the door, may seem febrile to contemporary readers. But it was precisely the poem's 'message' that excited Davidson's contemporaries. The admiration of the young Grant Richards, later Davidson's publisher but then working as W. T. Stead's assistant on the *Review of Reviews*, was characteristic of the response of young men of the time, for whom the poem was an exhilarating rejection of Victorian puritanism. William Archer was both impressed and perplexed by the poem and began a correspondence with Davidson that lasted for many years.

Through his association with the *Yellow Book* and the

[11] 'About Myself', *Candid Friend.*

Rhymers' Club, Davidson's name was frequently linked with the Decadence. There are certainly elements of *fin de siècle* Decadence in Davidson's exotic themes and exaggerated language. But even in 'A Ballad of a Nun', his verse is more forceful and robust, rhythmically and emotionally, than one finds in the work of Symons, Ernest Dowson, and other English admirers of the falling rhythms of Paul Verlaine and the French Symbolists. Davidson himself disliked the archetypal decadent poem of the 1890s, Dowson's 'Non sum qualis eram bonae sub regno Cynarae', which he thought overrated.[12] In many of his most successful lyrics from this period—in 'London', 'In Romney Marsh', 'In the Isle of Dogs'—the feeling rings or rises rhythmically at the end. At the same time, the sense of disconnection and age-end decay that haunts Davidson's ballads and songs is generally counterbalanced by the claims of ordinary human sympathies.

Many of Davidson's poems were based on earlier prose-accounts of his observations in and beyond London for the *Speaker* and the *Glasgow Herald* newspaper. His persona is that of the 'Random Itinerant'—his version of the wanderer and lover of nature celebrated in the writings of William Hazlitt, Thomas De Quincey, Walt Whitman, Richard Jefferies, and Robert Louis Stevenson. But, as in his *Fleet Street Eclogues*, his vagabond poet can discover the hidden truths of nature in the city as well as in the country. London may be the 'Bedlam of the universe' ('St Swithin's Day', l. 116), but it is also the place of imaginative human connections and identifications—in 'London', with its echoes of Wordsworth's 'On Westminster Bridge', the poet finds sympathetic communion with the human heart of the city; while in the Blakean monologue 'A Loafer', he gives a human voice to the insignificant tramp moving 'from eastern wretchedness | Through Fleet Street and the Strand' (ll. 13–14).

In urging Yeats and Rhymers in the early 1890s to have more 'blood and guts',[13] Davidson was voicing a northerner's impatience with over-refinement. But it was the ambivalence of his own attitude to his provincial Scottish background—opposed to its philistinism, while at the same time resisting certain aspects of cosmopolitan sophistication—that allowed his work to be

[12] 'A Perception', *Outlook*, 15 (1905), 951.

[13] Quoted in W. B. Yeats, *Autobiographies* (London, 1955).

identified with both the Decadence and the counter-Decadence. After 1895, the manly note of the counter-Decadence sounds more insistently in Davidson's work. His patriotic poems, with their imperialist pride in England as the foster-mother of nations, are unlikely to find a sympathetic audience today, but his celebration of Empire had little in common with the romantic conservatism of contemporaries like Alfred Austin, William Wallace, and Henry Newbolt. In 'Waiting', anger at the state of the nation's unemployed—'Prosperity's accustomed foil' (l. 15)—moves beyond any sentimental concerns in its call for strong leadership and the renewal of imperialist exploitation abroad. His sardonic, amoral approach to Empire has divided critics, who find his poetry both jingoistic and intolerant of the kind of feeling to which jingoistic poetry appeals.

A decisive event in Davidson's life and thought was his breakdown in 1896. It followed a year of crises and set-backs: his second series of *Fleet Street Eclogues* failed financially, and his hopes of a long run of his English adaptation of François Coppée's romantic melodrama *For the Crown* (1896), were disappointed when it closed after just over a hundred performances. Then in September his mother died. While in Edinburgh for the funeral, he worked on the proofs of his *New Ballads*, which contained his long narrative poem 'A Woman and her Son', in which an aggressively atheistic son tries to exorcise his dying mother's simple faith, only to fall victim to delirium and madness over her corpse. He himself had been close to breakdown for some time. At the height of his popularity during 1894 and 1895 he had found it difficult to cope with celebrity. Added to this was his ill health—like Joseph Conrad he suffered from bad teeth and poor nerves—the effects of his brother's mental breakdown, money and domestic worries, overwork, anxieties about ageing, and the burden of his mother's final illness. In December, without telling any of his friends, he left London for Shoreham on the south coast, near Brighton.

Shoreham proved to be a watershed in Davidson's poetic development. His middle-age crisis forced him into a deeper questioning of what he called 'the cat-call of the universe', the 'what' and 'why' of existence. He read Nietzsche in translation and delighted in his poetic conception of the 'superman'. It was Carlyle's hero-worship stripped of any of Carlyle's moralism. During the early months of 1898 he also read Ibsen and turned his thoughts to the problem of artistic personality, finally rejecting the notion of Romantic self-expression in favour of an enlarged view of the impersonal artist. He concluded that suffering was the universal insight that reconciles all great artists, and that it was only through an agonizing disintegration of the self that one gained insight into the truth of things. It was in these essentially aesthetic terms that he was able to reconcile himself finally to his breakdown and his sufferings. In his 'Eclogue: Votary and Artist', written that year, the artist is a prisoner in the Vale of Hinnom, a visceral hell where the mass of mankind, life's cast-offs and failures, are burned and ground into offal to sustain the beauty and harmony of the universe. It is a tragic vision of the world as irony, but the poem also contains suggestions of the heroic nature of the poet who in singing builds, 'A tabernacle even with these ghastly bones' (l. 218). Davidson moved back to London in August 1898, renting a small house at Streatham. His financial difficulties were eased when Edmund Gosse and William McCormick applied on his behalf for a Royal Literary Fund grant of £250.

His collections of *New Ballads* (1897) and *The Last Ballad, and Other Poems* (1899) did not enjoy the critical or financial success of his earlier *Ballads and Songs* (1894). Critics began to condemn the stridency which they felt marred the lyric passion of his verse, while there was uneasiness among conservative reviewers that traditional values were being threatened. It was a situation also experienced by other progressive artists in the 1890s, most notably by Thomas Hardy in the novel form, as art began to challenge the conventions and reticences of high Victorianism. Following the hostile reception of *The Last Ballad*, Davidson began to urge more aggressively the claims for a new kind of poetry. The targets of his attack were the inwardness and optimism of nineteenth-century verse. He wanted poetry to be democratized, and its subject-matter found in the newspaper and the street, and in the language of fact and science. He considered this to be a continuation of his own poetic practice, rather than a break with it. With the Pre-Raphaelite manifesto in mind, he called the new movement in poetry 'Pre-

Shakespearianism', claiming that Shakespeare had hung out a 'prismatic cloud . . . between the poets and the world'. His model 'Pre-Shakespearian' was James Thomson (1834–82), although it may be no coincidence that he had read Chaucer for the first time in 1898 in William McCormick's and A. W. Pollard's Globe edition of the *Works*, and embraced him enthusiastically as 'the first of the moderns'.[14] His conviction that the function of the poet might be to state the nature of the universe and man's place in it, rather than imply a criticism of life, provoked a heated debate in the press.

In the hope of a theatrical success, he accepted commissions for adaptations and wrote several original verse-dramas, but his real ambition now lay in the success of his poetry. The first fruits of his poetic manifesto were his blank-verse monologues, the Testaments, written beween 1901 and 1904, for those, in the words of his advertisement, 'who are not afraid to fathom what is subconscious in themselves and others'. From the first, critics recognized the ambition and scope of the Testaments, although there was strong antipathy to their irreligious message and their use of scientific material. Francis Thompson, who followed their publication with suspicion, finally denounced Davidson in the press as a poetic disciple of Nietzsche, a description that Davidson strenuously denied. Many of the ideas in the Testaments are to be found in his own early writings. The son's promise to make a heaven for 'mothers and their babes' in 'A Woman and her Son' is fulfilled, for instance, in the Empire-Builder's materialist vision of Heaven and Hell. The Testaments marry Davidson's secular inversion of Christian and pagan myths with ideas borrowed from Carlyle, Nietzsche, H. G. Wells, and popular scientific theorists of the day. The most important of these was Ernst Haeckel, the German zoologist, whose *The Riddle of the Universe* (1900) and *The Wonders of Life* (1904) postulated Matter as the one sole substance of the universe, interacting with an original primal ether to assume innumerable forms, including consciousness in man. Significantly Haeckel found an illustrious pedigree for his vital monism in Goethe and Wordsworth, who are often referred to as influences on Davidson's ideas. One important influence on the

[14] *A Rosary* (1903), 141.

Testaments, not generally recognized, was George Meredith's dissection of the mind of Napoleon in his 1898 *Odes in Contribution to the Song of French History*, although in his portraits of the man of strong mind, Davidson favoured the monologue form over Meredith's epic distance.

Davidson's relation with his speakers is a complex one. Initially he insisted on the dramatic nature of the poems, admitting that the materialist ideas were his own only after beginning *The Testament of a Prime Minister* in 1903. Although his reasons are not entirely clear, the evidence suggests that while he shared the materialist convictions of his speakers during the writing of the Testaments, he wanted to maintain a distinction between his personal morality and his speculative freedom as an artist. It is a crisis incorporated dramatically in the Testaments themselves, in which each of the speakers must struggle to suppress his common human responses to suffering and death. The crisis is most acute in *The Prime Minister*, who announces the Golden Age of Matter, of wealth as the final good—'Get Gold, get Gold; and be the Golden Age!' (l. 274)—only to be stricken with doubt in the middle of his speech to Parliament. The 'Tale of the Navvy' is told to him by one of the vagabonds he meets as he journeys in despair along the Thames. Drawn from the sensational police-stories of the day, it is Davidson's attempt to meet his own demand for poetry to take its subject-matter from the newspapers. Many reviewers objected to the ugliness of the incident—*The Times* compared it unfavourably with the dark elements in Dante, Shakespeare, and Lucretius—but Davidson himself believed that he had made 'one of the ugliest things that ever happened beautiful'.[15] The problems that troubled the early reviewers of the Testaments—the refusal to moralize, the impression of overall formlessness, and the eclectic combinations of dream-visions, myth, and allusion, with the language of scientific fact and contemporary reality—are more likely to be a source of pleasure for present-day readers, who have learned to respond to the synthesizing tendencies and impersonal vision of much twentieth-century verse, notably in Ezra Pound, T. S. Eliot, and the later Yeats.

Davidson intended to go on writing Testaments, but only one

[15] Letter to Grant Richards, 'Sunday' [Oct. 1904], Princeton University Library.

other, a Testament in his own name, appeared in 1908. With the box-office failure of his version of Victor Hugo's *Ruy Blas* in February 1904 he completed only his *Testament of a Prime Minister* before turning back to journalism to earn a livelihood. It proved to be blessing in disguise. His journalistic prose-accounts of his observations and journeys in and beyond London became the basis for his most important and original body of poems. His method of composition is the subject of 'The Aristocrat of the Road', where the 'stretch of pleasure ground' that the itinerant-poet reaches is poetry itself, in which experience and desire are finally reconciled. Though written in his late conversational manner, 'The Aristocrat of the Road' draws on ideas that can be found in his early London prose-writings.

Literary historians have tended to distinguish Davidson, the lyric poet of the 1890s from the later strident materialist of the Testaments and verse tragedies; but Davidson's poetic career does not divide so neatly. He continued to write lyrics—'A Runnable Stag' dates from 1905, a year in which he himself was surprised by the impulse to return to popular lyric forms. More significantly, his best poems after 1905 are, as Virginia Woolf noted, 'original without being prophetic',[16] developing in new technical and imaginative ways many of the themes and pre-occupations of his early work. In 'Fleet Street' the impressionistic spirit of his 'Random Itinerant' is aesthetically and intellectually enlarged by the defamiliarizing perspective of the materialist philosopher who experiences the oneness of matter in all its diverse forms. The linking of city scenes with natural landscapes in a single vision in 'London' and 'A Ballad in Blank Verse' finds new force in 'The Thames Embankment', where industrial debris and natural scenery merge in a Turneresque vision of light. His impulse to dramatic utterance is also given new direction in these later poems. In 'Two Dogs' he playfully combines Nietzschean ideas with the Burnsian tradition of animal impersonation, and brings the inanimate movingly to life in 'Snow'.

The modernity of these poems lies in large part in their abandonment of the human world. 'The Crystal Palace' opens

[16] Virginia Woolf, 'John Davidson', *Times Literary Supplement* (16 Aug. 1917), 390.

with the poet's irreverent vision of the 'temple of commercialism' and its directionless crowds as a grotesque parody of religious forms of assembly, but through its bizarre images of an object world and its featureless, primitive mob, the poem develops eerily towards an absence of any alternative human perspective that might give significance to the world. In 'London Bridge', the poet presents a similarly fantastic vision of the unreality of the station and the modern world which it serves. The humiliated man, the 'broken broker' at the end of the poem is like the poet himself, in a world that is less mysterious, but where fear of the primitive and unknown grows. These poems are among Davidson's most sustained individual achievements.

It is perhaps idle to speculate how Davidson might have developed as a poet if he had not ended his life prematurely. At the time of his death he had still to write the third and final play in his *God and Mammon* trilogy, a politicized version of the anti-Christian message contained in the Testaments. But it is possible that he had already embodied the imaginative conclusion to his materialist creed in *The Testament of John Davidson,* which he completed in August 1908, seven months before his death. The action of the poem, which is too close-textured to be represented adequately in a selection of his work, is a materialist revision of Keats's *Endymion* (1818) in which the character of 'John Davidson' seduces the virgin goddess Diana and so delivers men from the last remnant of deity and 'Other World'. Virgin worship—here, as in 'A Ballad of a Nun'—is seen to be the centre of the falsifying separation of body and soul that has lingered on in human thinking. Unlike the speakers of his other Testaments, the character of 'John Davidson' delivers himself both from fear of death and man's 'last Hell'—the belief that he himself is God. The poem ends with the anticipation of his suicide as the supreme act of fearlessness and self-mastery.

A clue to the direction Davidson's work might have taken if he had lived is perhaps to be found in 'Cain', which he intended to be one of a sequence of poems on biblical and historical figures—'Cain', 'Judas', 'Caesar Borgia', 'Calvin', and 'Cromwell'—under the general title 'When God Meant God'. The shift in focus is from those who deny God to those who quarrel with Him. Only 'Cain' was written, and he included it in *Fleet Street, and Other Poems* when he realized that it would be his last book.

When *Fleet Street, and Other Poems* appeared in 1909, the reviewers were generally bewildered by their strange cacophanies and juxtapositions and felt that Davidson had strayed further into the chopped-up prose and scientific jargon—'Davidsonese'—which they believed had swallowed up his lyric gift. Appreciation of Davidson's merits and originality as a poet, and of his anticipation of the direction that twentieth-century poetry was to take, had to wait. His growing reputation today is that of a poet of major significance whose place is within, yet whose presence enlarged, the traditions of English poetry.

The arrangement of the poems is basically chronological, although the date of publication has not always been followed. 'Piper, Play!', first published in 1898, was based on an earlier version written in 1887, when Davidson was a schoolmaster in Crieff. It is included here among his early poems. Three other poems—'In the Isle of Dogs', 'Holiday at Hampton Court', and 'A Northern Suburb'—are based on prose accounts of Davidson's early London experiences and are here grouped with the other poems from the period of *A Random Itinerary* and *Ballad and Songs* with which they belong in spirit and manner. I have also placed all of the *Fleet Street* poems, except 'Cain', before *The Testament of John Davidson*, in the order of the prose versions on which they were based. The dates of the prose writings are given in the brief notes to the poems. Davidson's manuscripts of *The Testament of John Davidson* and *Fleet Street, and Other Poems* are at Princeton University Library. Where an earlier variant to the final published version of the poems has been preferred, this is indicated in the footnotes. For the prose extract on 'Rhyme', Davidson's earlier version has been preferred to his extensive revision which appeared as 'On Poetry' in *Holiday, and Other Poems.*

Bibliography

DAVIDSON'S WRITINGS

(*The place of publication is London unless otherwise stated.*)

POETRY

Diabolus Amans: A Dramatic Poem (Glasgow: Wilson & McCormick, 1885).

In a Music-Hall, and Other Poems (Ward & Downey, 1891).

Fleet Street Eclogues. First series (Elkin Mathews and John Lane, 1893).

Ballads and Songs (John Lane, 1894).

St. George's Day: A Fleet Street Eclogue (John Lane, 1895).

Fleet Street Eclogues. Second series (John Lane, 1896).

New Ballads (John Lane, 1897).

The Last Ballad, and Other Poems (John Lane, 1899).

The Testament of a Vivisector (Grant Richards, 1901).

The Testament of a Man Forbid (Grant Richards, 1901).

The Testament of an Empire-Builder (Grant Richards, 1902).

A Rosary (Grant Richards, 1903) (a miscellany of prose and verse).

The Testament of a Prime Minister (Grant Richards, 1904).

Selected Poems (John Lane, 1905).

Holiday, and Other Poems (E. Grant Richards, 1906).

The Testament of John Davidson (Grant Richards, 1908).

Fleet Street, and Other Poems (Grant Richards, 1909).

PLAYS

Bruce: A Drama in Five Acts (Wilson & McCormick, 1886).

Smith: A Tragedy (Glasgow: Frederick W. Wilson & Brother, 1888).

Plays (privately printed, Greenock, 1889), containing *An Unhistorica Pastoral, A Romantic Farce,* and *Scaramouch in Naxos*; reissued with a new title-page as *Scaramouch in Naxos: A Pantomime, and Other Plays* by T. Fisher Unwin (1890); reissued with same title but new imprin by Mathews and Lane (1893).

Plays (Elkin Mathews and John Lane, 1894), containing *Bruce* and *Smith,* in addition to the plays already published in his *Plays* o 1889.

For the Crown (Nassau Press, 1896) (his adaptation of Françoi Coppée's verse drama *Pour la couronne*).

Godfrida: A Play in Four Acts (John Lane, 1898).

Self's the Man: A Tragi-Comedy (Grant Richards, 1901).

The Knight of the Maypole: A Comedy in Four Acts (Grant Richards, 1903)

A Queen's Romance (Grant Richards, 1904) (his adaptation of Victor Hugo's *Ruy Blas*).

The Theatrocrat: A Tragic Play of Church and Stage (E. Grant Richards, 1905).

God and Mammon: A Trilogy, 1: *The Triumph of Mammon* (Grant Richards, 1907).

God and Mammon: A Trilogy, 2: *Mammon and his Message* (Grant Richards, 1908).

FICTION

The North Wall (Wilson & McCormick: Glasgow, 1885).

Perfervid: The Career of Ninian Jamieson (Ward & Downey, 1890).

The Great Men and *A Practical Novelist* (Ward & Downey, 1891) (*The Great Men* is a collection of stories and sketches; *A Practical Novelist* is *The North Wall* retitled).

Baptist Lake (Ward & Downey, 1894).

A Full and True Account of the Wonderful Mission of Earl Lavender (Ward & Downey, 1895).

Miss Armstrong's and Other Circumstances (Methuen & Co., 1896) (a collection of stories).

In collaboration with C. J. Wills:

Was He Justified? (Spencer Blackett, 1891).

Jardyne's Wife (3 vols.; Trischler and Co., 1891).

His Sister's Hand (3 vols.; Griffith & Farran, 1892).

Laura Ruthven's Widowhood (3 vols.; Lawrence & Bullen, 1892).

An Easy-Going Fellow (Chatto & Windus, 1896).

MISCELLANEOUS PROSE

Persian Letters (2 vols.; privately printed [John C. Nimmo], 1892) (a translation of Charles Louis, Baron de Montesquieu's *Lettres persanes*).

Sentences and Paragraphs (Lawrence & Bullen, 1893).

A Random Itinerary (Elkin Mathews and John Lane, 1894).

A Rosary (Grant Richards, 1903) (a miscellany of prose and verse).

SECONDARY LITERATURE

(For a check-list of writings about Davidson, see Mary O'Connor's 'John Davidson: An Annotated Bibliography of Writings about Him', *English Literature in Transition*, 20 (1977), 112–74.)

Crawford, Robert, *Devolving English Literature* (Oxford, 1992).

Fineman, Hayim, *John Davidson: A Study of the Relation of his Ideas to his Poetry* (Philadelphia, 1916).

Lester, John A., jun., 'Friedrich Nietzsche and John Davidson: A Study in Influence', *Journal of the History of Ideas*, 18 (1957), 411–29.

—— 'Prose–Poetry Transmutation in the Poetry of John Davidson', *Modern Philology*, 56 (1958), 38–44.

O'Connor, Mary, *John Davidson* (Edinburgh, 1987).

Townsend, J. Benjamin, *John Davidson: Poet of Armageddon* (New Haven, Conn., 1961).

Turnbull, Andrew, Introduction to *The Poems of John Davidson* (Edinburgh, 1973).

Biographical Outline

1857	Born 11 April, at Barrhead, Renfrewshire, fourth child and eldest son of Alexander Davidson and Helen Crocket.
1860	His father becomes assistant to James Morison, leader of the Evangelical Union, in Glasgow; the family moves there until 1862, when Alexander Davidson becomes pastor at Greenock.
1871–6	John interrupts his schooling at the Highlander's Academy, Greenock, where he has been a pupil since the age of 8, to work at Walker's Sugar Company (1871) and the Public Analyst's Office (1872); returns to the Highlander's Academy as pupil-teacher (1873–6).
1876–7	Matriculates at Edinburgh University in November 1876, but leaves the following year, after one session, and takes up his first teaching post at Alexander's Charity School, Glasgow.
1878–84	Leaves Alexander's Charity School in March 1878 after meeting Swinburne at Professor John Nichol's house; his hopes of living off his poetry come to nothing. Works as a schoolmaster: Perth Academy (1878–81); Kelvinside Academy (1881–2); Hutcheson's Charity School, Paisley (1883–4).
1884	Works as a clerk in Glasgow office of Clark's, a Paisley thread-firm; writes his 'In a Music-Hall' poems.
1885	Returns to teaching at Morrison's Academy, Crieff; the Glasgow publishers Wilson & McCormick publish his first book, the novel *The North Wall*, dedicated to Margaret McArthur, daughter of a Perth bobbin-manufacturer. They marry on 23 October.
1886	Publication of his Scottish chronicle-play *Bruce*.
1887	Alexander (Sandy) born 19 December; on 22 December receives a term's notice of dismissal following conflict with the rector, George Strathairn.
1888	Moves back to Greenock; publication of his spasmodic verse-drama *Smith: a Tragedy*.
1889	Menzies born 29 March; Davidson's younger sister Lizzie dies on 15 May; issues his *Plays* privately and visits London for three months.
1890	Finds work in London as a journalist and as a collaborator with the novelist C. J. Wills; moves with his family to a

house in the north London suburb of Hornsey; his *Plays* reissued as *Scaramouch in Naxos* by T. Fisher Unwin. Ward and Downey publish *Perfervid: The Career of Ninian Jamieson.*

1891 His father dies in December; publication of *In a Music-Hall, and Other Poems.*

1892 Publication of his translation of Montesquieu's *Lettres persanes*; his name appears as joint author, with C. J. Wills, of the three-volume novel *Laura Ruthven's Widowhood.*

1893 His brother Thomas spends six months at Morningside Asylum, Edinburgh, following a mental breakdown. Publication of *Fleet Street Eclogues*, first series, and *Sentences and Paragraphs*, a collection of essays and aphorisms.

1894 Publication of *A Random Itinerary* (travel sketches), *Baptist Lake* (a novel), and a new collected edition of his *Plays*; contributes to the *Yellow Book*; has success with *Ballads and Songs.*

1895 Sons sent to a farm near Brighton for health reasons; he and his wife move to a flat in Warrington Crescent. Publication of his novel *Earl Lavender.*

1896 Publication of *Fleet Street Eclogues*, second series, and *Miss Armstrong's, and Other Circumstances* (stories); *For the Crown*, his adaptation of the French writer François Coppée's successful melodrama *Pour la couronne*, has a disappointing run at the Lyceum. His mother dies in September; he moves to Shoreham, near Brighton, in December, following breakdown in health.

1897 Publication of *New Ballads*; *The Children of the King*, his version of Ernst Rosmer's *Königskinder*, has a short run at the Court theatre during October and December.

1898 Returns to London in autumn, taking a house at Streatham; receives Royal Literary Fund grant for £250. His romantic verse-drama *Godfrida* published but never performed.

1899 His article on 'Pre-Shakespearianism' in the *Speaker* causes controversy; publication of *The Last Ballad, and Other Poems.*

1901 His new publisher, Grant Richards, issues his unacted tragicomedy *Self's the Man* and two of his proposed series of Testaments—*The Testament of a Vivisector* and *The Testament of a Man Forbid.*

1902 Publication of *The Testament of an Empire-Builder.*

1903 Publication of *The Knight of the Maypole*, a romantic comedy, written for the American impresario Charles Frohman but never performed, and *A Rosary*, a miscellany of verse and prose.

1904 Publication of *The Testament of a Prime Minister*, *A Queen's Romance*, his adaptation of Victor Hugo's *Ruy Blas*, with Mrs Patrick Campbell playing opposite Lewis Waller, closes after only two weeks.

1905 Returns to journalism; publication of his blank-verse tragedy *The Theatrocrat*; John Lane issues a *Selected Poems*.

1906 Receives £250 from G. B. Shaw to write an original play: 'The Game of Life' is neither published nor performed. Awarded a Civil List pension of £100 a year. Publication of *Holiday, and Other Poems*.

1907 Publication of *The Triumph of Mammon*, the first part of a dramatic verse trilogy *God and Mammon*; moves to Penzance.

1908 Publication of *The Testament of John Davidson* and *Mammon and his Message*, the second part of his trilogy; begins but abandons the third part; becomes reader of manuscripts for Richards.

1909 Disappears 23 March; body found at sea in September; coroner's verdict 'Found Dead'; buried at sea 21 September. *Fleet Street, and Other Poems* published posthumously.

POETRY
SIX EARLY POEMS

1
Ayrshire Jock[1]

I, John Auld, in my garret here,
  In Sauchiehall Street, Glasgow, write,
Or scribble, for my writing-gear
  Is sadly worn: a dirty white
  My ink is watered to; and quite
Splay-footed is my pen—the handle
  Bitten into a brush; my light,
Half of a ha'penny tallow-candle.

A little fire is in the grate,
  Between the dusty bars, all red—
All black above: the proper state
  To last until I go to bed.
  I have a night-cap on my head,
And one smokes in a tumbler by me:
  Since heart and brain are nearly dead,
Who would these comforters deny me?

Ghosts lurk about the glimmering room,
  And scarce-heard whispers hoarsely fall:
I fear no more the rustling gloom,
  Nor shadows moving on the wall;
  For I have met at church and stall,
In streets and road, in graveyards dreary,
  The quick and dead, and know them all:
Nor sight nor sound can make me eerie.[2]

Midnight rang out an hour ago;
  Gone is the traffic in the street,
Or deadened by the cloak of snow
  The gallant north casts at the feet
  Of merry Christmas, as is meet;

[1] This satire on Burnsian imitation was probably written when D. was a member of Prof. John Nichol's circle at Glasgow University in the late 1870s and early 1880s. The poem appeared in *In a Music-Hall, and Other Poems.*

[2] *eerie*: afraid (Scots).

With icicles the gutter bristles;
  The wind that blows now slack, now fleet,
In every muffled chimney whistles.

I'll draw the blind and shut—alas!
  No shutters here! . . . My waning sight
Sees through the naked windows pass
  A vision. Far within the night
  A rough-cast cottage, creamy white,
With drooping eaves that need no gutters,
  Flashes its bronze thatch in the light,
And flaps its old-style, sea-green shutters.

There I was born. . . . I'll turn my back;
  I would not see my boyhood's days:
When later scenes my memories track,
  Into the magic pane I'll gaze.
  Hillo! the genial film of haze
Is globed and streaming on my tumbler:
  It's getting cold; but this I'll praise,
Though I'm a universal grumbler.

Now, here's a health to rich and poor,
  To lords and to the common flock,
To priests, and prigs, and—to be sure!—
  Drink to yourself, old Ayrshire Jock;
  And here's to rhyme, my stock and rock;
And though you've played me many a plisky,[3]
  And had me in the prisoner's dock,
Here's my respects t'ye, Scottish whisky!

That's good! To get this golden juice
  I starve myself and go threadbare.
What matter though my life be loose?
  Few know me now, and fewer care.
  Like many another lad from Ayr—
This is a fact, and all may know it—
  And many a Scotchman everywhere,
Whisky and Burns made me a poet.

[3] *plisky*: trick (Scots).

Just as the penny dreadfuls make
The 'prentice rob his master's till,
Ploughboys their honest work forsake,
Inspired by Robert Burns. They swill
Whisky like him, and rhyme; but still
Success attends on imitation
Of faults alone: to drink a gill
Is easier than to stir a nation.

They drink, and write their senseless rhymes,
Tagged echoes of the lad of Kyle,
In mongrel Scotch: didactic times
In Englishing our Scottish style
Have yet but scotched it: in a while
Our bonny dialects may fade hence:
And who will dare to coin a smile
At those who grieve for their decadence?

These rhymesters end in scavenging,
Or carrying coals, or breaking stones;
But I am of a stronger wing,
And never racked my brains or bones.
I rhymed in English, catching tones
From Shelley and his great successors;
Then in reply to written groans,
There came kind letters from professors.

With these, and names of lords as well,
My patrons, I brought out my book;
And—here's my secret—sold, and sell
The same from door to door. I look
My age; and yet, since I forsook
Ploughing for poetry, my income
Comes from my book, by hook or crook;
So I have found the muses winsome.

That last rhyme's bad, the pun is worse;
But still the fact remains the same;
My book puts money in my purse,
Although it never brought me fame.

I once desired to make a name,
But hawking daily an edition
Of one's own poetry would tame
The very loftiest ambition.

Ah! here's my magic looking-glass!
Against the panes night visions throng.
Lo! there again I see it pass,
My boyhood! Ugh! The kettle's song
Is pleasanter, so I'll prolong
The night an hour yet. Soul and body!
There's surely nothing very wrong
In one more glass of whisky toddy!

2

The Rev. Habakkuk McGruther, of Cape Wrath, in 1879[1]

God save old Scotland! Such a cry
  Comes raving north from Edinburgh.
It shakes the earth, and rends the sky,
  It thrills and fills true hearts with sorrow.
'There's no such place, by God's good grace,
  As smoky hell's dusk-flaming cavern?'
Ye fools, beware, or ye may share
  The hottest brew of Satan's tavern.

Ye surely know that Scotland's fate
  Controls the whole wide-world's well-being;
And well ye know her godly state
  Depends on faith in sin's hell-feeing.[2]
And would ye then, false-hearted men,
  From Scotland rape her dear damnation?
Take from her hell, then take as well
  From space the law of gravitation.

A battle-cry for every session
  In these wild-whirling, heaving last days:
'Discard for ever the Confession;
  Abolish, if you choose, the Fast-days;
Let Bible knowledge in school and college
  No more be taught—we'll say, 'All's well.'
'Twill scarcely grieve us, if you but leave us
  For Scotland's use, in Heaven's name, Hell.'

[1] According to R. M. Wenley, in the introd. to his *Poems by John Davidson* (New York, 1924), the background to this poem was the controversial Robertson Smith case of 1878–81. William Robertson Smith, Professor of Oriental Languages and Old Testament Exegesis at the Free Church College in Aberdeen, was examined by the Free Church Assembly for heresy after applying the methods of 'Higher Criticism' in his contribution to the ninth edition of the *Encyclopaedia Britannica.* He was acquitted but was eventually deprived of his post in 1881. The poem appeared in *In a Music-Hall, and Other Poems,* and in George Douglas's anthology of *Contemporary Scottish Verse* (London, 1893).

[2] *feeing*: wages (Scots).

3

Thoreau[1]

I tell you who mock my behaviour,
  There is not a desert in space;
Each insect and moss is a saviour,
  And Nature is one thing with Grace.

Who called me a hermit misprized me;
  I never renounced a desire;
The thought of the world has disguised me,
  And clad with a vapour my fire.

But soon in the night of my dying
  The pillar of cloud will be lit,
And the dark world, ashamed of its lying,
  Behold I am fairer than it.

'He is terrible; no one can love him;
  His virtue is bloodless and cold;
He thinks there is no soul above him;
  His birthright it was to be old.'

O scandalous wordling, self-centred,
  Can you love what you cannot descry
With a vision the light never entered?
  Is your conscience less dreadful than I?

Close-sucking the bone and the marrow
  Where life is the sweetest, I fed
Like an eagle, while you, like a sparrow,
  Hop, hunting the streets for your bread.

As freshly as at the beginning,
  The earth in green garments arrayed,

[1] This poem is difficult to date. It was probably written in the early 1880s. An alternative date is 1889, when D. corresponded with Dr A. H. Japp, whose *Thoreau: His Life and Aims* (London, 1878), written under his pseudonym of H. A. Page, may have inspired the poem. The poem appeared in *In a Music-Hall, and Other Poems.*

In the dance of the universe spinning,
  A pregnant, immaculate maid,

Looks up with her forehead of mountains,
  And shakes the pine-scent from her hair,
And laughs with the voice of her fountains,
  A pagan, as savage as fair.

4
Selene Eden,[1] *from* In a Music-Hall

My dearest lovers know me not;
  I hide my life and soul from sight;
I conquer all whose blood is hot;
  My mystery is my mail of might.

I had a troupe who danced with me:
  I veiled myself from head to foot;
My girls were nude as they dared be;
  They sang a chorus, I was mute.

But now I fill the widest stage
  Alone, unveiled, without a song;
And still with mystery I engage
  The aching senses of the throng.

A dark-blue vest with stars of gold,
  My only diamond in my hair,
An Indian scarf about me rolled:
  That is the dress I always wear.

And first the sensuous music whets
  The lustful crowd; the dim-lit room
Recalls delights, recalls regrets;
  And then I enter in the gloom.

I glide, I trip, I run, I spin,
  Lapped in the lime-light's aureole.
Hushed are the voices, hushed the din,
  I see men's eyes like glowing coal.

My loosened scarf in odours drenched
  Showers keener hints of sensual bliss;

[1] This is the fifth of the six 'In a Music-Hall' monologues which provided the title for D.'s first published collection of verse in 1891. The sequence was written in 1884, when D. was working as a clerk in Glasgow. 'Selene Eden' was selected for inclusion in George Douglas's *Contemporary Scottish Verse* (London, 1893).

The music swoons, the light is quenched,
  Into the dark I blow a kiss.

Then, like a long wave rolling home,
  The music gathers speed and sound;
I, dancing, am the music's foam,
  And wilder, fleeter, higher bound,

And fling my feet above my head;
  The light grows, none aside may glance;
Crimson and amber, green and red,
  In blinding baths of these I dance.

And soft, and sweet, and calm, my face
  Looks pure as unsunned chastity,
Even in the whirling triple pace:
  That is my conquering mystery.

5

Piper, Play![1]

Now the furnaces are out,
  And the aching anvils sleep;
Down the road the grimy rout
  Tramples homeward twenty deep.
    Piper, play! Piper, play!
      Though we be o'erlaboured men,
    Ripe for rest, pipe your best!
      Let us foot it once again!

Bridled looms delay their din;
  All the humming wheels are spent;
Busy spindles cease to spin;
  Warp and woof must rest content.
    Piper, play! Piper, play!
      For a little we are free!
    Foot it girls and shake your curls,
      Haggard creatures though we be!

Racked and soiled the faded air
  Freshens in our holiday;
Clouds and tides our respite share;
  Breezes linger by the way.
    Piper, rest! Piper, rest!
      Now, a carol of the moon!
    Piper, piper, play your best!
      Melt the sun into your tune!

We are of the humblest grade;
  Yet we dare to dance our fill:
Male and female were we made—
  Fathers, mothers, lovers still!
    Piper—softly; soft and low;

[1] An early version of this was written to be sung by the pupils of Morrison's Academy, Crieff, where D. was an English master from 1885 to 1888. It was first published in the *Daily Chronicle* (18 Dec. 1895), 5, and was included in *New Ballads*.

Pipe of love in mellow notes,
Till the tears begin to flow,
And our hearts are in our throats!

Nameless as the stars of night
Far in galaxies unfurled,
Yet we wield unrivalled might,
Joints and hinges of the world!
Night and day! night and day!
Sound the song the hours rehearse!
Work and play! work and play!
The order of the universe!

Now the furnaces are out,
And the aching anvils sleep;
Down the road a merry rout
Dances homeward, twenty deep.
Piper, play! Piper, play!
Wearied people though we be,
Ripe for rest, pipe your best!
For a little we are free!

6

'The Boat is Chafing', *from* Scaramouch in Naxos[1]

The boat is chafing at our long delay,
  And we must leave too soon
The spicy sea-pinks and the inborne spray,
  The tawny sands, the moon.

Keep us, O Thetis,[2] in our western flight!
  Watch from thy pearly throne
Our vessel, plunging deeper into night
  To reach a land unknown.

[1] The pantomime *Scaramouch in Naxos* was written in Crieff in 1888 and published in *Plays* (Greenock, 1889); this was reissued in London by T. Fisher Unwin as *Scaramouch in Naxos* the following year.

[2] Greek sea-goddess and mother of Achilles.

POEMS

1892–1909

7

From Fleet Street Eclogues, first series[1]

[Eulogy of the Daisy], *from* Good Friday[2]

The vanguards of the daisies come,
  Summer's crusaders sanguine-stained,
The only flowers that left their home
  When happiness in Eden reigned.

They strayed abroad, old writers tell,
  Hardy and bold, east, west, south, north:
Our guilty parents, when they fell,
  And flaming vengeance drove them forth,

Their haggard eyes in vain to God,
  To all the stars of heaven turned;
But when they saw where in the sod,
  The golden-hearted daisies burned,

Sweet thoughts that still within them dwelt
  Awoke, and tears embalmed their smart;
On Eden's daisies couched they felt
  They carried Eden in their heart.

[1] These are from the first cycle of seven poems which D. began writing in 1892. They were published by Elkin Mathews and John Lane in 1893.

[2] The speaker is Menzies, who has returned to London after a visit to the country.

St Swithin's Day[1]

BASIL

We four—since Easter-time we have not met.

BRIAN

And now the Dog Days bake us in our rooms
Like heretics in Dis's[2] lidded tombs.

SANDY

Oh, for a little wind, a little wet!

BRIAN

A little wet, but not from heaven, I pray!
Have you forgotten 'tis St Swithin's Day?

BASIL

Cast books aside, strew paper, drop the pen!
Bring ice, bring lemons, bring St Julien![3]

SANDY

Bring garlands!

BRIAN

With the laurel, lest it fade,
Let Bacchus twist vine-leaf and cabbage-blade!

BASIL

I would I lay beside a brook at morn,
And watched the shepherd's-clock declare the hours;
And heard the husky whisper of the corn,
Legions of bees in leagues of summer flowers.

BRIAN

Who has been out of London?

BASIL

Once, in June

[1] There is a legend that if it rains on St Swithin's Day (15 July), it will do so for forty succeeding days. Lines 19–48 are based on Richard Jefferies, 'The Coming of Summer', *Longman's Magazine* (19 Dec. 1891), 137–47, and first appeared in the *Speaker*, 4 (12 Dec. 1891), 713–14, as 'In the Hollow at Long Ditton'.

[2] God of the underworld (classical mythology).

[3] Wine of the Beaujolais region.

Upstream I went to hear the summer tune
The birds sing at Long Ditton[4] in a vale
Sacred to him who wrote his own heart's tale.[5]
Of singing birds that hollow is the haunt:
Never was such a place for singing in!
The valley overflows with song and chaunt,
And brimming echoes spill the pleasant din.
High in the oak-trees where the fresh leaves sprout,
The blackbirds with their oboe voices make
The sweetest broken music all about
The beauty of the day for beauty's sake,
The wanton shadow and the languid cloud,
The grass-green velvet where the daisies crowd;
And all about the air that softly comes
Thridding the hedgerows with its noiseless feet,
The purling waves with muffled elfin drums,
That step along their pebble-paven street;
And all about the mates whose love they won,
And all about the sunlight and the sun.
The thrushes into song more bravely launch
Than thrushes do in any other dell;
Warblers and willow-wrens on every branch,
Each hidden by a leaf, their rapture tell;
Green-finches in the elms sweet nothings say,
Busy with love from dawn to dusk are they.
A passionate nightingale adown the lane
Shakes with the force and volume of his song
A hawthorn's heaving foliage; such a strain,
Self-caged like him to make his singing strong,
Some poet may have made in days of yore,
Untold, unwritten, lost for evermore.

SANDY

Your holiday was of a rarer mood,
A dedication loftier than mine;
But yet I swear my holiday was good:
I went to Glasgow just for auld lang syne.

[4] Rural village on the Thames.

[5] Richard Jefferies, who wrote the autobiographical *The Story of My Heart* (1883).

In Sauchiehall Street[6] in the afternoon
I saw a lady walking all in black,
But on her head a hat shaped like the moon,
Crescent and white and clouded with a veil.
I could not see if she were fair or pale
Because her beauty hid her like a mist:
But well I knew her bosom from her back;
And all her delicacy well I wist:
And every boy and man that saw her pass
Adored the beauty of that Scottish lass.
I said within: 'Three things are worthiest knowing,
And when I know them nothing else I know.
I know unboundedly, what needs no showing,
That women are most beautiful; and then
I know I love them; and I know again
Herein alone true Science lies, for, lo!
Old Rome's a ruin; Caesar is a name;
The Church?—alas! a lifeboat, warped and sunk;
God, a disputed title: but the fame
Of those who sang of love, fresher than spring,
Blossoms for ever with the tree of life,
Whose boughs are generations; and its trunk
Love; and its flowers, lovers.'

BRIAN

Love we sing,
Towards Love we strive; no other song or strife
We know, or heed.—You, Menzies, what say you?
Dark, in your corner—with a volume too!

MENZIES

Now that I hang above the loathsome hell
Of smouldering spite and foul disparagement,
Even as a Christian, singed and basted well
By Christians, hung in dreadful discontent
Chained to a beam, and dangling in the fire;
And like an ocean-searching sailor-wight
Whose lonely eyes and clinging fingers tire;
And like a desperate, pallid acolyte

[6] A busy shopping-street in Glasgow.

Of giddy Fortune, who with straining clutch
Swings in her wheel's wind from its lower rim,
Doubting of all things, disbelieving much,
I come to him who sang the heavenly hymn.

BRIAN

To Colin Clout! But whence this desperate thought?

MENZIES

Two months ago I published—

BRIAN

(Out! Alack!)

MENZIES

A book that held the essence of my life:
Wrong praise and wrong abuse was all I got.

BASIL

We all have suffered from the critic's knife.

SANDY

And helpless lain on many a weekly rack.

MENZIES

But I am weak.

BASIL

No, Menzies; you are strong.
Already you have cast aside the wrong,
And solace found in Spenser's noble song.
When I was in like case it took a year
Before my wounds were whole, my vision clear.

MENZIES

What brought you to yourself?

BASIL

I prayed.

MENZIES

Indeed!

BRIAN

To whom?

BASIL

I know not; 'tis the mood I need—
Submissive aspiration.

MENZIES

Pray with us:
Here from the city's centre make appeal.

BRIAN

Where hawkers cry, where roar the cab and 'bus.

BASIL

So be it. On your knees, then: Sandy, kneel.—

Sweet powers of righteousness protect us now!
Your adversary, Fate, has driven us down
From that green-crowned, sun-fronting mountain-brow,
Where peace and aspiration (ebb and flow
Of thought that strives to whelm the infinite;
And, as the sun for ever fails to drown
More than a little hollow of the night,
Pierces a rush-light's ray's length into it)
Swung our ecstatic spirits to and fro
Between the Heaven and Hades of delight,
Down to that bedlam of the universe,
That sepulchre of souls for ever yawning,
That jug of asps—God's enemy, Time's hearse,
The world, that blister raised by every dawning.
Help, ere it drive us mad, this devil's din!
The clash of iron, and the clink of gold;
The quack's, the beggar's whining manifold;
The harlot's whisper, tempting men to sin;
The voice of priests who damn each other's missions;
The babel-tongues of foolish politicians,
Who shout around a swaying Government;
The groans of beasts of burden, mostly men,
Who toil to please a thankless upper ten;
The knowledge-monger's cry, 'A brand-new fact!'
The dog's hushed howl from whom the fact was rent;
The still-voice 'Culture'; and the slogan 'Act!'
Save us from madness; keep us night and day,
Sweet powers of righteousness to whom we pray.

Christmas Eve[1]

SANDY
In holly hedges starving birds
  Silently mourn the setting year.

BASIL
Upright like silver-plated swords
  The flags stand in the frozen mere.

BRIAN
The mistletoe we still adore
  Upon the twisted hawthorn grows.

MENZIES
In antique gardens hellebore
  Puts forth its blushing Christmas rose.

SANDY
Shrivelled and purple, cheek by jowl,
  The hips and haws hang drearily.

BASIL
Rolled in a ball the sulky owl
  Creeps far into his hollow tree.

BRIAN
In abbeys and cathedrals dim
  The birth of Christ is acted o'er;
The kings of Cologne worship Him,
  Balthazar, Jasper, Melchior.

MENZIES
And while our midnight talk is made
  Of this and that and now and then,
The old earth-stopper with his spade
  And lantern seeks the fox's den.

[1] This is the concluding Eclogue in the sequence. D. later published the ballad separately in *Ballads and Songs* as 'A Ballad of Hell', with a note that it would not be reprinted in *Fleet Street Eclogues*. The Eclogue is here restored to its original form.

SANDY

Oh, for a northern blast to blow
   These depths of air that cream and curdle!

BASIL

Now are the halcyon days, you know;
   Old Time has leapt another hurdle;

And pauses as he only may
   Who knows he never can be caught.

BRIAN

The winter solstice, shortest day
   And longest night, was past I thought.

BASIL

Oh yes! but fore-and-aft a week
   Silent the winds must ever be,
Because the happy halcyons seek
   Their nests upon the sea.

BRIAN

The Christmas-time! the lovely things
   That last of it! Sweet thoughts and deeds!

SANDY

How strong and green old legend clings
   Like ivy round the ruined creeds!

MENZIES

A fearless, ruthless, wanton band,
   Deep in our hearts we guard from scathe,
Of last year's log, a smouldering brand
   To light at Yule the fire of faith.

BRIAN

The shepherds in the field at night
   Beheld an angel glory-clad,
And shrank away with sore affright.
   'Be not afraid,' the angel bade.

'I bring good news to king and clown,
   To you here crouching on the sward;

For there is born in David's town
  A Saviour, which is Christ the Lord.

'Behold the babe is swathed, and laid
  Within a manger.' Straight there stood
Beside the angel all arrayed
  A heavenly multitude.

'Glory to God', they sang; 'and peace,
  Good pleasure among men.'

SANDY

The wondrous message of release!

MENZIES

  Glory to God again!

BRIAN

Again! God help us to be good!

BASIL

  Hush! hark! Without; the waits, the waits![2]
With brass, and strings, and mellow wood.

MENZIES

  A simple tune can ope heaven's gates!

SANDY

Slowly they play, poor careful souls,
  With wistful thoughts of Christmas cheer,
Unwitting how their music rolls
  Away the burden of the year

BASIL

And with the charm, the homely rune,
  Our thoughts like childhood's thoughts are given,
When all our pulses beat in tune
  With all the stars of heaven.

MENZIES

Oh cease! Oh cease!

[2] *waits*: band of street musicians at Christmas who sing and play carols.

SANDY

Ay, cease; and bring
The wassail-bowl, the cup of grace.

BRIAN

Pour wine, and heat it till it sing.
With cloves and cardamums and mace.

BASIL

And frothed and sweetened round it goes,
While some one tells a winter's tale.

MENZIES

I have one—not of winter's snows;
Of flames it is.

SANDY

Tell it.

BASIL

All hail!

MENZIES

'A letter from my love to-day!
Oh, unexpected, dear appeal!'
She struck a happy tear away,
And broke the crimson seal.

'My love, there is no help on earth,
No help in heaven; the dead-man's bell
Must toll our wedding; our first hearth
Must be the well-paved floor of hell.'

Her colour died from out her face,
Her eyes like ghostly candles shone;
She cast dread looks about the place,
And clenched her teeth, and read right on.

'I must not pass the prison door;
Here must I rot from day to day,
Unless I wed whom I abhor,
My cousin, Blanche of Valencay.

'At midnight with my dagger keen
  I'll take my life; it must be so.
Meet me in hell to-night, my queen,
  For weal and woe.'

She laughed although her face was wan,
  She girded on her golden belt,
She took her jewelled ivory fan,
  And at her glowing missal knelt.

Then rose, 'And am I mad?' she said;
  She broke her fan, her belt untied;
With leather girt herself instead,
  And stuck a dagger at her side.

She waited, shuddering in her room,
  Till sleep had fallen on all the house.
She never flinched; she faced her doom:
  They two must sin to keep their vows.

Then out into the night she went;
  And stooping, crept by hedge and tree;
Her rose-bush flung a snare of scent,
  And caught a happy memory.

She fell, and lay a minute's space;
  She tore the sward in her distress;
The dewy grass refreshed her face;
  She rose and ran with lifted dress.

She started like a morn-caught ghost
  Once when the moon came out and stood
To watch; the naked road she crossed,
  And dived into the murmuring wood.

The branches snatched her streaming cloak;
  A live thing shrieked; she made no stay!
She hurried to the trysting-oak—
  Right well she knew the way.

Without a pause she bared her breast,
  And drove her dagger home and fell,

And lay like one that takes her rest,
  And died and wakened up in hell.

She bathed her spirit in the flame,
  And near the centre took her post;
From all sides to her ears there came,
  The dreary anguish of the lost.

The devil started at her side,
  Comely, and tall, and black as jet.
'I am young Malespina's bride;
  Has he come hither yet?'

'My poppet, welcome to your bed.'
  'Is Malespina here?'
'Not he! To-morrow he must wed
  His cousin Blanche, my dear!'

'You lie, he died with me to-night.'
  'Not he! it was a plot.' 'You lie.'
'My dear, I never lie outright.'
  'We died at midnight, he and I.'

The devil went. Without a groan
  She, gathered up in one fierce prayer,
Took root in hell's midst all alone,
  And waited for him there.

She dared to make herself at home
  Amidst the wail, the uneasy stir.
The blood-stained flame that filled the dome,
  Scentless and silent, shrouded her.

How long she stayed I cannot tell;
  But when she felt his perfidy,
She marched across the floor of hell;
  And all the damned stood up to see.

The devil stopped her at the brink:
  She shook him off; she cried, 'Away!'

'My dear, you have gone mad, I think.'
'I was betrayed: I will not stay.'

Across the weltering deep she ran—
A stranger thing was never seen:
The damned stood silent to a man;
They saw the great gulf set between.

To her it seemed a meadow fair;
And flowers sprang up about her feet;
She entered heaven; she climbed the stair;
And knelt down at the mercy-seat.

Seraphs and saints with one great voice
Welcomed that soul that knew not fear;
Amazed to find it could rejoice,
Hell raised a hoarse half-human cheer.

BRIAN

Hush! hark! the waits, far up the street!

BASIL

A distant, ghostly charm unfolds
Of magic music wild and sweet,
Anomes and clarigolds.

8
Holiday at Hampton Court[1]

Scales of pearly cloud inlay
  North and south the turquoise sky,
While the diamond lamp of day
  Quenchless burns, and time on high
A moment halts upon his way
  Bidding noon again good-bye.

Gaffers, gammers,[2] huzzies,[3] louts,
  Couples, gangs, and families
Sprawling, shake, with Babel-shouts
  Bluff King Hal's funereal trees;
And eddying groups of stare-abouts
  Quiz the sandstone Hercules.

When their tongues and tempers tire,
  Harry and his little lot
Condescendingly admire
  Lozenge-bed and crescent-plot,
Aglow with links of azure fire,
  Pansy and forget-me-not.

Where the emerald shadows rest
  In the lofty woodland aisle,
Chaffing lovers quaintly dressed
  Chase and double many a mile,
Indifferent exiles in the west
  Making love in cockney style.

Now the echoing palace fills;
  Men and women, girls and boys,
Trample past the swords and frills,
  Kings and Queens and trulls and toys;

[1] Based on a prose article, 'Whit-Monday at Hampton Court', *Speaker*, 7 (27 May 1893), 598–9. The poem appeared in the *Speaker*, 18 (23 July 1898), 110, and in *The Last Ballad*.

[2] *gammers*: older women (from 'grandmother').

[3] *huzzies*: girls (jocular).

Or listening loll on window-sills,
  Happy amateurs of noise!

That for pictured rooms of state!
  Out they hurry, wench and knave,
Where beyond the palace-gate
  Dusty legions swarm and rave,
With laughter, shriek, inane debate,
  Kentish fire and comic stave.

Voices from the river call;
  Organs hammer tune on tune;
Larks triumphant over all
  Herald twilight coming soon,
For as the sun begins to fall
  Near the zenith gleams the moon.

9

In the Isle of Dogs[1]

While the water-wagon's ringing showers
Sweetened the dust with a woodland smell,
'Past noon, past noon, two sultry hours',
Drowsily fell
From the schoolhouse clock
In the Isle of Dogs by Millwall Dock.

Mirrored in shadowy windows draped
With ragged net or half-drawn blind
Bowsprits, masts, exactly shaped
To woo or fight the wind,
Like monitors of guilt
By strength and beauty sent,
Disgraced the shameful houses built
To furnish rent.

From the pavements and the roofs
In shimmering volumes wound
The wrinkled heat;
Distant hammers, wheels and hoofs,
A turbulent pulse of sound,
Southward obscurely beat,
The only utterance of the afternoon,
Till on a sudden in the silent street
An organ-man drew up and ground
The Old Hundredth tune.[2]

Forthwith the pillar of cloud that hides the past
Burst into flame,
Whose alchemy transmuted house and mast,
Street, dockyard, pier and pile:
By magic sound the Isle of Dogs became

[1] Based on a 'Random Itinerary' article, 'The Isle of Dogs to Sydenham', *Glasgow Herald* (22 July 1893), 4. The poem appeared in the *Speaker*, 18 (13 Aug. 1898), 204, and in *The Last Ballad.*

[2] Hymn tune set to Psalm 100 in the Geneva psalter of 1551.

A northern isle[3]—
A green isle like a beryl set
In a wine-coloured sea,
Shadowed by mountains where a river met
The ocean's arm extended royally.

There also in the evening on the shore
An old man ground the Old Hundredth tune,
An old enchanter steeped in human lore,
Sad-eyed, with whitening beard, and visage lank:
Not since and not before,
Under the sunset or the mellowing moon,
Has any hand of man's conveyed
Such meaning in the turning of a crank.

Sometimes he played
As if his box had been
An organ in an abbey richly lit;
For when the dark invaded day's demesne,
And the sun set in crimson and in gold;
When idlers swarmed upon the esplanade,
And a late steamer wheeling towards the quay
Struck founts of silver from the darkling sea,
The solemn tune arose and shook and rolled
Above the throng,
Above the hum and tramp and bravely knit
All hearts in common memories of song.

Sometimes he played at speed;
Then the Old Hundredth like a devil's mass
Instinct with evil thought and evil deed,
Rang out in anguish and remorse. Alas!
That men must know both Heaven and Hell!
Sometimes the melody
Sang with the murmuring surge;
And with the winds would tell
Of peaceful graves and of the passing bell.
Sometimes it pealed across the bay

[3] Bute, where D. went on family holidays as a boy.

A high triumphal dirge,
A dirge
For the departing undefeated day.

A noble tune, a high becoming mate
Of the capped mountains and the deep broad firth;
A simple tune and great,
The fittest utterance of the voice of earth.

10

A Cinque Port[1]

Below the down the stranded town,
  What may betide forlornly waits,
With memories of smoky skies,
  When Gallic navies crossed the straits;
When waves with fire and blood grew bright,
And cannon thundered through the night.

With swinging stride the rhythmic tide
  Bore to the harbour barque and sloop;
Across the bar the ship of war,
  In castled stern and lanterned poop,
Came up with conquests on her lee,
The stately mistress of the sea.

Where argosies have wooed the breeze,
  The simple sheep are feeding now;
And near and far across the bar
  The ploughman whistles at the plough;
Where once the long waves washed the shore,
Larks from their lowly lodgings soar.

Below the down the stranded town
  Hears far away the rollers beat;
About the wall the seabirds call;
  The salt wind murmurs through the street;
Forlorn the sea's forsaken bride,
Awaits the end that shall betide.

[1] The Cinque Ports were originally the five coastal towns of Hastings, Romney, Hythe, Dover, and Sandwich, whose responsibility it was in early times to provide shipping for the state. D. visited the south coast several times in the early months of 1894. The poem was first published as 'Song of a Cinque Port' in the *Pall Mall Gazette* (2 Mar. 1894), 2, and appeared in *Ballads and Songs*.

11

In Romney Marsh[1]

As I went down to Dymchurch Wall,
  I heard the South sing o'er the land;
I saw the yellow sunlight fall
  On knolls where Norman churches stand.

And ringing shrilly, taut and lithe,
  Within the wind a core of sound,
The wire from Romney town to Hythe
  Alone its airy journey wound.

A veil of purple vapour flowed
  And trailed its fringe along the Straits;
The upper air like sapphire glowed;
  And roses filled Heaven's central gates.

Masts in the offing wagged their tops;
  The swinging waves pealed on the shore;
The saffron beach, all diamond drops
  And beads of surge, prolonged the roar.

As I came up from Dymchurch Wall,
  I saw above the Downs' low crest
The crimson brands of sunset fall,
  Flicker and fade from out the west.

Night sank: like flakes of silver fire
  The stars in one great shower came down;
Shrill blew the wind; and shrill the wire
  Rang out from Hythe to Romney town.

The darkly shining salt sea drops
  Streamed as the waves clashed on the shore;
The beach, with all its organ stops
  Pealing again, prolonged the roar.

[1] Based on a prose article, 'Romney Marsh', *Glasgow Herald* (3 Mar. 1894), 4. The poem appeared in the *Speaker*, 9 (17 Mar. 1894), 308, and in *Ballads and Songs*.

12

Two Songs[1]

London

Athwart the sky a lowly sigh
  From west to east the sweet wind carried;
The sun stood still on Primrose Hill;
  His light in all the city tarried;
The clouds on viewless columns bloomed
Like smouldering lilies unconsumed.

'Oh sweetheart, see! how shadowy,
  Of some occult magician's rearing,
Or swung in space of heaven's grace
  Dissolving, dimly reappearing,
Afloat upon ethereal tides
St. Paul's above the city rides!'

A rumour broke through the thin smoke
  Enwreathing abbey, tower, and palace,
The parks, the squares, the thoroughfares,
  The million-peopled lanes and alleys,
An ever-muttering prisoned storm,
The heart of London beating warm.

[1] These appeared together in the first issue of the *Yellow Book* in April 1894. They were later reprinted separately in *Ballads and Songs* as 'London' and 'Spring III' respectively.

Down-a-Down

Foxes peeped from out their dens;
  Day grew pale and olden;
Blackbirds, willow-warblers, wrens
  Staunched their voices golden.

High, oh high, from the opal sky,
  Shouting against the dark,
'Why, why, why must the days go by?'
  Fell a passionate lark.

But the cuckoos beat their brazen gongs,
  Sounding, sounding, so;
And the nightingales poured in starry songs
  A galaxy below.

Slowly tolling, the vesper bell
  Ushered the shadowy night:
Down-a-down in a hawthorn dell
  A boy and a girl and love's delight.

13
From Spring[1]

By lichened tree and mossy plinth
  Like living flames of purple fire,
Flooding the wood, the hyacinth
  Uprears its heavy-scented spire.

The redstart shakes its crimson plume,
  Singing alone till evening's fall
Beside the pied and homely bloom
  Of wallflower on the crumbling wall.

Now dandelions light the way,
  Expecting summer's near approach;
And, bearing lanterns night and day,
  The great marsh-marigolds keep watch.

[1] Originally as 'Spring IV' in *Ballads and Songs.*

14

A Northern Suburb[1]

Nature selects the longest way,
And winds about in tortuous grooves;
A thousand years the oaks decay;
The wrinkled glacier hardly moves.

But here the whetted fangs of change
Daily devour the old demesne—
The busy farm, the quiet grange,
The wayside inn, the village green.

In gaudy yellow brick and red,
With rooting pipes, like creepers rank,
The shoddy terraces o'erspread
Meadow, and garth, and daisied bank.

With shelves for rooms the houses crowd,
Like draughty cupboards in a row—
Ice-chests when wintry winds are loud,
Ovens when summer breezes blow.

Roused by the fee'd policeman's knock,
And sad that day should come again,
Under the stars the workmen flock
In haste to reach the workmen's train.

For here dwell those who must fulfil
Dull tasks in uncongenial spheres,
Who toil through dread of coming ill,
And not with hope of happier years—

The lowly folk who scarcely dare
Conceive themselves perhaps misplaced,
Whose prize for unremitting care
Is only not to be disgraced.

[1] Based on a prose article, 'A Suburban Philosopher', *Glasgow Herald* (22 Apr. 1893), 9. The poem appeared in the *Speaker*, 13 (9 May 1896), 509–10, and in *New Ballads*.

15
Thirty Bob a Week[1]

I couldn't touch a stop and turn a screw,
And set the blooming world a-work for me,
Like such as cut their teeth—I hope, like you—
On the handle of a skeleton gold key;
I cut mine on a leek, which I eat it every week:
I'm a clerk at thirty bob as you can see.

But I don't allow it's luck and all a toss;
There's no such thing as being starred and crossed;
It's just the power of some to be a boss,
And the bally power of others to be bossed:
I face the music, sir; you bet I ain't a cur;
Strike me lucky if I don't believe I'm lost!

For like a mole I journey in the dark,
A-travelling along the underground
From my Pillar'd Halls and broad Suburbean Park,
To come the daily dull official round;
And home again at night with my pipe all alight,
A-scheming how to count ten bob a pound.

And it's often very cold and very wet,
And my missis stitches towels for a hunks;[2]
And the Pillar'd Halls is half of it to let—
Three rooms about the size of travelling trunks,
And we cough, my wife and I, to dislocate a sigh,
When the noisy little kids are in their bunks.

But you never hear her do a growl or whine,
For she's made of flint and roses, very odd;
And I've got to cut my meaning rather fine,
Or I'd blubber, for I'm made of greens and sod:

[1] This appeared in the second volume of the *Yellow Book* in July 1894, and in *Ballads and Songs*.

[2] *a hunks*: a crusty old miser. D. may well have had in mind here the woman 'plying her needle and thread' in Thomas Hood's 'The Song of the Shirt'.

So p'r'aps we are in Hell for all that I can tell,
And lost and damn'd and served up hot to God.

I ain't blaspheming, Mr. Silver-tongue;
I'm saying things a bit beyond your art:
Of all the rummy starts you ever sprung,
Thirty bob a week's the rummiest start!
With your science and your books and your the'ries about spooks,
Did you ever hear of looking in your heart?

I didn't mean your pocket, Mr., no:
I mean that having children and a wife,
With thirty bob on which to come and go,
Isn't dancing to the tabor and the fife:
When it doesn't make you drink, by Heaven! it makes you think,
And notice curious items about life.

I step into my heart and there I meet
A god-almighty devil singing small,
Who would like to shout and whistle in the street,
And squelch the passers flat against the wall;
If the whole world was a cake he had the power to take,
He would take it, ask for more, and eat them all.

And I meet a sort of simpleton beside,
The kind that life is always giving beans;
With thirty bob a week to keep a bride
He fell in love and married in his teens:
At thirty bob he stuck; but he knows it isn't luck:
He knows the seas are deeper than tureens.

And the god-almighty devil and the fool
That meet me in the High Street on the strike,
When I walk about my heart a-gathering wool,
Are my good and evil angels if you like.
And both of them together in every kind of weather
Ride me like a double-seated bike.

That's rough a bit and needs its meaning curled.
  But I have a high old hot un in my mind—
A most engrugious[3] notion of the world,
  That leaves your lightning 'rithmetic behind:
I give it at a glance when I say 'There ain't no chance,
  Nor nothing of the lucky-lottery kind.'

And it's this way that I make it out to be:
  No fathers, mothers, countries, climates—none;
Not Adam was responsible for me,
  Nor society, nor systems, nary one:
A little sleeping seed, I woke—I did, indeed—
  A million years before the blooming sun.

I woke because I thought the time had come;
  Beyond my will there was no other cause;
And everywhere I found myself at home,
  Because I chose to be the thing I was;
And in whatever shape of mollusc or of ape
  I always went according to the laws.

I was the love that chose my mother out;
  I joined two lives and from the union burst;
My weakness and my strength without a doubt
  Are mine alone forever from the first:
It's just the very same with a difference in the name
  As 'Thy will be done.' You say it if you durst!

They say it daily up and down the land
  As easy as you take a drink, it's true;
But the difficultest go to understand,
  And the difficultest job a man can do,
Is to come it brave and meek with thirty bob a week,
  And feel that that's the proper thing for you.

It's a naked child against a hungry wolf;
  It's playing bowls upon a splitting wreck;

[3] *engrugious*: Andrew Turnbull in *The Poems of John Davidson* (Edinburgh, 1973) suggests that this is D.'s comic version of 'egregious'.

It's walking on a string across a gulf
With millstones fore-and-aft about your neck;
But the thing is daily done by many and many a one;
And we fall, face forward, fighting, on the deck.

16

A Ballad of a Nun[1]

From Eastertide to Eastertide
 For ten long years her patient knees
Engraved the stones—the fittest bride
 Of Christ in all the diocese.

She conquered every earthly lust;
 The abbess loved her more and more;
And, as a mark of perfect trust,
 Made her the keeper of the door.

High on a hill the convent hung,
 Across a duchy looking down,
Where everlasting mountains flung
 Their shadows over tower and town.

The jewels of their lofty snows
 In constellations flashed at night;
Above their crests the moon arose;
 The deep earth shuddered with delight.

Long ere she left her cloudy bed,
 Still dreaming in the orient land,
On many a mountain's happy head
 Dawn lightly laid her rosy hand.

The adventurous sun took Heaven by storm;
 Clouds scattered largesses of rain;
The sounding cities, rich and warm,
 Smouldered and glittered in the plain.

[1] Most likely written in the summer of 1894 when H. Rider Haggard entered into an acrimonious correspondence with the secretary of the Catholic Truth Society in the pages of the *Pall Mall Gazette*, following Haggard's comments in a footnote to his novel *Montezuma's Daughter* (1893) on the subject of the immuring of nuns. There are several versions of the story, but D.'s most likely source is Viller de L'Isle-Adam's short story 'Sœur Natalia' in his *Nouveaux contes cruels* of 1888. The poem appeared in the *Yellow Book* in Oct. 1894, and in *Ballads and Songs*.

Sometimes it was a wandering wind,
  Sometimes the fragrance of the pine,
Sometimes the thought how others sinned,
  That turned her sweet blood into wine.

Sometimes she heard a serenade
  Complaining sweetly far away:
She said, 'A young man woos a maid';
  And dreamt of love till break of day.

Then would she ply her knotted scourge
  Until she swooned; but evermore
She had the same red sin to purge,
  Poor, passionate keeper of the door!

For still night's starry scroll unfurled,
  And still the day came like a flood:
It was the greatness of the world
  That made her long to use her blood.

In winter-time when Lent drew nigh,
  And hill and plain were wrapped in snow,
She watched beneath the frosty sky
  The nearest city nightly glow.

Like peals of airy bells outworn
  Faint laughter died above her head
In gusts of broken music borne:
  'They keep the Carnival', she said.

Her hungry heart devoured the town:
  'Heaven save me by a miracle!
Unless God sends an angel down,
  Thither I go though it were Hell.'

She dug her nails deep in her breast,
  Sobbed, shrieked, and straight withdrew the bar:
A fledgling flying from the nest,
  A pale moth rushing to a star.

Fillet and veil in strips she tore;
  Her golden tresses floated wide;
The ring and bracelet that she wore
  As Christ's betrothed, she cast aside.

'Life's dearest meaning I shall probe;
  Lo! I shall taste of love at last!
Away!' She doffed her outer robe,
  And sent it sailing down the blast.

Her body seemed to warm the wind;
  With bleeding feet o'er ice she ran:
'I leave the righteous God behind;
  I go to worship sinful man.'

She reached the sounding city's gate;
  No question did the warder ask:
He passed her in: 'Welcome, wild mate!'
  He thought her some fantastic mask.

Half-naked through the town she went;
  Each footstep left a bloody mark;
Crowds followed her with looks intent;
  Her bright eyes made the torches dark.

Alone and watching in the street
  There stood a grave youth nobly dressed;
To him she knelt and kissed his feet;
  Her face her great desire confessed.

Straight to his house the nun he led:
  'Strange lady, what would you with me?'
'Your love, your love, sweet lord', she said;
  'I bring you my virginity.'

He healed her bosom with a kiss;
  She gave him all her passion's hoard;
And sobbed and murmured ever, 'This
  Is life's great meaning, dear, my lord.

'I care not for my broken vow;
  Though God should come in thunder soon,
I am sister to the mountains now,
  And sister to the sun and moon.'

Through all the towns of Belmarie
  She made a progress like a queen.
'She is', they said, 'whate'er she be,
  The strangest woman ever seen.

'From fairyland she must have come,
  Or else she is a mermaiden.'
Some said she was a ghoul, and some
  A heathen goddess born again.

But soon her fire to ashes burned;
  Her beauty changed to haggardness;
Her golden hair to silver turned;
  The hour came of her last caress.

At midnight from her lonely bed
  She rose, and said, 'I have had my will.'
The old ragged robe she donned, and fled
  Back to the convent on the hill.

Half-naked as she went before,
  She hurried to the city wall,
Unnoticed in the rush and roar
  And splendour of the carnival.

No question did the warder ask:
  Her ragged robe, her shrunken limb,
Her dreadful eyes! 'It is no mask;
  It is a she-wolf, gaunt and grim!'

She ran across the icy plain;
  Her worn blood curdled in the blast;
Each footstep left a crimson stain;
  The white-faced moon looked on aghast.

She said between her chattering jaws,
'Deep peace is mine, I cease to strive;
Oh, comfortable convent laws,
That bury foolish nuns alive!

'A trowel for my passing-bell,
A little bed within the wall,
A coverlet of stones; how well
I there shall keep the Carnival!'

Like tired bells chiming in their sleep,
The wind faint peals of laughter bore;
She stopped her ears and climbed the steep,
And thundered at the convent door.

It opened straight: she entered in,
And at the wardress' feet fell prone:
'I come to purge away my sin;
Bury me, close me up in stone.'

The wardress raised her tenderly;
She touched her wet and fast-shut eyes:
'Look, sister; sister, look at me;
Look; can you see through my disguise?'

She looked and saw her own sad face,
And trembled, wondering, 'Who are thou?'
'God sent me down to fill your place:
I am the Virgin Mary now.'

And with the word, God's mother shone:
The wanderer whispered, 'Mary, hail!'
The vision helped her to put on
Bracelet and fillet, ring and veil.

'You are sister to the mountains now,
And sister to the day and night;
Sister to God.' And on the brow
She kissed her thrice, and left her sight.

While dreaming in her cloudy bed,
  Far in the crimson orient land,
On many a mountain's happy head
  Dawn lightly laid her rosy hand.

17

From A Ballad in Blank Verse of the Making of a Poet[1]

[His Father's House]

His father's house looked out across a firth
Broad-bosomed like a mere, beside a town[2]
Far in the North, where Time could take his ease,
And Change hold holiday; where Old and New
Weltered upon the border of the world.

'Oh now', he thought—a youth whose sultry eyes,
Bold brow and wanton mouth were not all lust,
But haunted from within and from without
By memories, visions, hopes, divine desires—
'Now may my life beat out upon this shore
A prouder music than the winds and waves
Can compass in their haughtiest moods. I need
No world more spacious than the region here:
The foam-embroidered firth, a purple path
For argosies that still on pinions speed,
Or fiery-hearted cleave with iron limbs
And bows precipitous the pliant sea;
The sloping shores that fringe the velvet tides
With heavy bullion and with golden lace
Of restless pebble woven and fine spun sand;
The villages that sleep the winter through,
And, wakening with the spring, keep festival
All summer and all autumn: this grey town
That pipes the morning up before the lark
With shrieking steam, and from a hundred stalks
Lacquers the sooty sky; where hammers clang
On iron hulls, and cranes in harbours creak
Rattle and swing, whole cargoes on their necks;

[1] First appeared in *Ballads and Songs.* D. revised and improved it for his *Selected Poems* of 1905, where the title was shortened to 'A Ballad in Blank Verse'.

[2] Greenock, Scotland.

Where men sweat gold that others hoard or spend,
And lurk like vermin in their narrow streets:
This old grey town, this firth, the further strand
Spangled with hamlets, and the wooded steeps,
Whose rocky tops behind each other press,
Fantastically carved like antique helms
High-hung in heaven's cloudy armoury,
Is world enough for me. Here daily dawn
Burns through the smoky east; with fire-shod feet
The sun treads heaven, and steps from hill to hill
Downward before the night that still pursues
His crimson wake; here winter plies his craft,
Soldering the years with ice; here spring appears,
Caught in a leafless brake, her garland torn,
Breathless with wonder, and the tears half-dried
Upon her rosy cheek; here summer comes
And wastes his passion like a prodigal
Right royally; and here her golden gains
Free-handed as a harlot autumn spends;
And here are men to know, women to love.'

His father, woman-hearted, great of soul,
Wilful and proud, save for one little shrine
That held a pinch-beck cross, had closed and barred
The many mansions of his intellect.

'My son', he said—to him, fresh from his firth
And dreams at evening; while his mother sat,
She also with her dingy crucifix
And feeble rushlight, praying for her boy—
'My son, have you decided for the Lord?
Your mother's heart and mine are exercised
For your salvation. Will you turn to Christ?
Now, young and strong, you hanker for the world;
But think: the longest life must end at last,
And then come Death and Judgment. Are you fit
To meet your God before the great white throne?
If on the instant Death should summon you,
What doom would the Eternal Judge pronounce—
"Depart from me", or "Sit on My right hand?"

In life it is your privilege to choose,
But after death you have no choice at all.
Die unbelieving, and in endless woe
You must believe throughout eternity.
My son, reject not Christ; he pleads through me;
The Holy Spirit uses my poor words.
How it would fill your mother's heart and mine,
And God's great heart with joy unspeakable,
Were you, a helpless sinner, now to cry,
"Lord I believe: help Thou mine unbelief."'
He clenched his teeth; his blood, fulfilled of brine,
Of sunset, and his dreams, boomed in his ears.
A vision rose before him; and the sound
Husky and plaintive of his father's voice
Seemed unintelligible and afar.
He saw Apollo on the Dardan beach:
The waves lay still; the winds hung motionless,
And held their breath to hear the rebel god,
Conquered and doomed, with stormy sobbing song,
And crashing discords of his golden lyre,
Reluctantly compel the walls of Troy,
Unquarried and unhewn, in supple lines
And massive strength to rise above the town.

[His Rebellion]

Slowly he broke his mother's tender heart,
Until she died in anguish for his sins.
His father then besought him on his knees,
With tears and broken speech and pleading hands

'My son', he said, 'you open all the wounds
Daily and nightly of the Lord of Heaven:
You killed your mother, you are killing me:
Is it not sin enough, poor foolish boy?'

For this was in the North, where Time stands still
And Change holds holiday, where Old and New
Welter upon the border of the world,
And savage faith works woe.

'Oh, let me be!'
The dreamer cried, and rushing from the house
He sought the outcast Aphrodite, dull,
Tawdry, unbeautiful, but still divine
Even in the dark streets of a noisome port.

At times he wrote his dreams, rebellious still
That he should be constrained to please himself
As one is eased by roaring on the rack.
Desperate he grew, and wandering by his firth,
Exclaimed against the literature he loved.
'Lies, lies!' he muttered. 'And the noblest, lies!
Why should we lie? what penalty is this—
To write, and sing, and think, and speculate,
Hag-ridden by ideas, or 'twixt the shafts
Like broken horses, blinded, bitted, reined,
And whipped about the world by steel-tagged creeds!'

Wasted and sad with wantonness, and wan
With fantasy—a furnace seven times hot,
Wherein he tried all things; and wrung with woe
To see his father dying for his sake,

And by the memory of his mother's death,
He yielded tamely and professed himself
Convinced of sin but confident in Christ.

Then to the table of the Lord he went,
Ghastly, with haunted eyes that shone, and limbs
That scarcely bore him, like a heretic
Led to the chamber where tormentors stood
Muffled and silent, earnest to explore,
With cunning flames and cords and engines dire,
The sunken wells of pain, the gloomy gulfs
Obscurely wallowing in the souls of men.

In solemn tones the grey-haired presbyter—
'This is My Body which is given for you,
This do in memory of Me.'

The boy,
Whose blood within him clamoured like a storm,
Uttered a smothered cry and rose, but lo!
The happy triumph on his father's face!
'Why do I not die now? like husks of corn,
The bread, like vitriol the sip of wine!
I eat and drink damnation to myself
To give my father's troubled spirit peace.'
The stealthy elders creaked about the floor,
Guiding the cup and platter; looking down,
The children in the gallery smirked and watched
Who took the deepest draught; and ancient dames
Crumpled their folded handkerchiefs, and pressed
With knuckly fingers sprays of southernwood.

Ah! down no silver beam the Holy Grail
Glided from Heaven, a crimson cup that throbbed
As throbs the heart divine; no aching sounds
Of scarce-heard music stole into the aisle,
Like disembodied pulses beating love.

But in the evening by the purple firth
He walked, and saw brown locks upon the brine,

And pale hands beckon him to come away,
Where mermaids, with their harps and golden combs,
Sit throned upon the carven antique poops
Of treasure-ships, and soft sea-dirges sing
Over the green-gilt bones of mariners.
He saw vast forms and dreadful draw aside
The flowing crimson curtains of the west
With far-off thundrous rustle, and threaten him
From heaven's porch; beneath his feet the earth
Quaked like a flame-sapped bridge that spans the wave
Of fiery Phlegethon;[1] and in the wind
An icy voice was borne from some waste place,
Piercing him to the marrow. Night came down,
And still he wandered helpless by the firth,
That under clouded skies gleamed black and smooth
Like cooling pitch. But when the moon broke out,
And poured athwart the glittering ebony
Torrents of molten silver, hurtling thoughts
Trooped forth disorderly.

'I'll have no creed',
He said. 'Though I be weakest of my kind,
I'll have no creed. Lo! there is but one creed,
The vulture-phoenix that for ever tears
The soul of man in chains of flesh and blood
Rivetted to the earth; the clime, the time,
Change but its plumage. Gluttonous bird of prey,
More fatal than all famines, plagues and wars,
I wrench you off, although my soul go too!
With bloody claws and dripping beak unfleshed,
Spread out your crackling vans that darken heaven;
Rabid and curst, fly yelping where you list!
Henceforth I shall be God; for consciousness
Is God: I suffer; I am God: this Self,
That all the universe combines to quell,
Is greater than the universe; and *I*
Am that I am. To think and not be God?—
It cannot be! Lo! I shall spread this news,

[1] A river of fire encircling the infernal regions (classical mythology).

And gather to myself a band of Gods—
An army, and go forth against the world,
Conquering and to conquer. Snowy steppes
Of Muscovy, frost-bound Siberian plains,
And scalding sands of Ethiopia,
Where groans oppress the bosom of the wind,
And men in gangs are driven to icy graves,
Or lashed to brutish slavery under suns
Whose sheer beams scorch and flay like
    burning blades,
Shall ring, enfranchised, with divine delight.
At home, where millions mope, in labyrinths
Of hideous streets astray without a clue,
Unfed, unsexed, unsoulled, unhelped, I bring
Life, with the gospel, "Up, quit you like Gods!"'

[The Making of a Poet]

He stood beside the house a little space,
Hearing the wind speak low in whispers quaint,
An irresponsible and wandering voice.
But soon he hastened to the water's edge;
For from the shore there came sea-minstrelsy
Of waves that broke upon the hollow beach,
With liquid sound of pearling surges blent,
Cymbals, and muffled drums and dulcimers.

Sparse diamonds in the dead-black dome of night,
A few stars lit the moon-deserted air
And swarthy heaving of the firth obscure.
He, knowing every rock and sandy reach,
All night unfalteringly walked the shore,
While tempest after tempest rose and fell
Within his soul, that like an o'er-wrought sea
Laboured to burst its continent and hang
Some glittering trophy high among the stars.
At last the fugal music of the tide,
With cymbals, muffled drums, and dulcimers,
Into his blood a rhythmic measure beat,
And gave his passion scope and way in words.

'How unintelligent, how blind am I,
How vain!' he cried. 'A God? a mole, a worm!
An engine frail, of brittle bones conjoined;
With tissue packed; with nerves, transmitting force;
And driven by water, thick and coloured red:
That may for some few pence a day be hired
In thousands to be shot at! Oh, a God,
That lies and steals and murders! Such a God!
Passionate, dissolute, incontinent!
A God that starves in thousands, and ashamed!
Or shameless in the workhouse lurks; that sweats
In mines and foundries! An enchanted God,
Whose nostrils in a palace breathe perfume,
Whose cracking shoulders hold the palace up,

Whose shoeless feet are rotting in the mire!
A God who said a little while a go,
"I'll have no creed"; and of his Godhead straight
Patched up a creed unwittingly—with which
He went and killed his father. Subtle lie
That tempts our weakness always; magical,
And magically changed to suit the time!
"Lo, ye shall be as Gods!"—the serpent's cry—
Rose up again, "Ye shall be sons of God";
And now the glosing[1] word is in the air,
"Thou shalt be God by simply taking thought."
And if one could, believing this, convert
A million to be upright, chaste and strong,
Gentle and tolerant, it were but to found
A new religion, bringing new offence,
Setting the child against the father still.
Some thought imprisons us; we set about
To bring the world within the woven spell:
Our ruthless creeds that bathe the earth in blood
Are moods by alchemy made dogmas of—
The petrifaction of a metaphor.
No creed for me! I am a man apart:
A mouthpiece for the creeds of all the world;
A soulless life that angels may possess
Or demons haunt, wherein the foulest things
May loll at ease beside the loveliest;
A martyr for all mundane moods to tear;
The slave of every passion; and the slave
Of heat and cold, of darkness and of light;
A trembling lyre for every wind to sound.
I am a man set by to overhear
The inner harmony, the very tune
Of Nature's heart; to be a thoroughfare
For all the pageantry of Time; to catch
The mutterings of the Spirit of the Hour
And make them known; and of the lowliest
To be the minister, and therefore reign
Prince of the powers of the air, lord of the world

[1] *glosing*: deceiving, specious.

And master of the sea. Within my heart
I'll gather all the universe, and sing
As sweetly as the spheres; and I shall be
The first of men to understand himself.
And lo! to give me courage comes the dawn,
Crimsoning the smoky east; and still the sun
With fire-shod feet shall step from hill to hill
Downward before the night; winter shall ply
His ancient craft, soldering the years with ice;
And spring appear, caught in a leafless brake,
Breathless with wonder and the tears half-dried
Upon her rosy cheek; summer shall come
And waste his passion like a prodigal
Right royally; and autumn spend her gold
Free-handed as a harlot; men to know,
Women to love are waiting everywhere.'

18
To My Friend[1]

What is between us two, we know:
Shake hands and let the whole world go.

19
To My Enemy[2]

Unwilling friend, let not your spite abate:
Help me with scorn, and strengthen me with hate.

[1] The friend was Richard Le Gallienne, who, as a reader of manuscripts for Mathews and Lane, recommended that they publish *Fleet Street Eclogues.* Le Gallienne reviewed the volume warmly in 'Books and Bookmen', *Star* (4 May 1893), 2, and in 'Pan in Fleet Street', *Daily Chronicle* (6 May 1893), 3. The couplet introduced *Ballads and Songs.*

[2] This follows 'To My Friend' in *Ballads and Songs.*

20

A Loafer[1]

I hang about the streets all day,
All night I hang about;
I sleep a little when I may,
But rise betimes the morning's scout;
For through the year I always hear
Afar, aloft, a ghostly shout.

My clothes are worn to threads and loops;
My skin shows here and there;
About my face like seaweed droops
My tangled beard, my tangled hair;
From cavernous and shaggy brows
My stony eyes untroubled stare.

I move from eastern wretchedness
Through Fleet Street and the Strand;
And as the pleasant people press
I touch them softly with my hand,
Perhaps to know that still I go
Alive about a living land.

For, far in front the clouds are riven;
I hear the ghostly cry,
As if a still voice fell from heaven
To where sea-whelmed the drowned folks lie
In sepulchres no tempest stirs
And only eyeless things pass by.

In Piccadilly spirits pass:
Oh, eyes and cheeks that glow!
Oh, strength and comeliness! Alas,
The lustrous health is earth I know
From shrinking eyes that recognise
No brother in my rags and woe.

[1] This street song appeared in *Ballads and Songs.*

I know no handicraft, no art,
  But I have conquered fate;
For I have chosen the better part,
  And neither hope, nor fear, nor hate.
With placid breath on pain and death,
  My certain alms, alone I wait.

And daily, nightly comes the call,
  The pale, unechoing note,
The faint 'Aha!' sent from the wall
  Of heaven, but from no ruddy throat
Of human breed or seraph's seed,
  A phantom voice that cries by rote.

21

[Confessions of a Haunted Mind], *from* Lammas[1]

It was engraven deeply on my mind
In daily lessons from my infancy
Until I left my father's house, that not
Ability and knowledge, beauty and strength,
But goodness only can avail. I watched,
And thought I understood that beauty, strength
And knowledge ought to reign, they being indeed
The trinity of goodness; but I claimed
That this should be revealed to me, that I
Should be directly warned by God Himself
In the old fashion. Strange it seems; and yet
It was not very strange. Each morn and eve,
Year after year, I heard the prophets read,
Heard strong believing prayer: the atmosphere
Was not allied more nearly to my breath
Than to my mind the thought of God—no dream
Of deity; a living, active God.
On hill-tops, by the sea, in storm, in calm
I cried to Him to speak to me; with tears
Solicited a sign. Sleepless and pale
I wandered like a ghost, and day and night
Waited upon a message from on high.
Sunset and sunrise came; the seasons past;
The years went slowly by; but still to me
The universe was dumb. Books helped me not,
Except for pleasure or to gain command
Of words: I would have God's own voice or none.
At last I ceased to hope and found content
In roaming through the land. The magic sun
Drew pictures on my sight. Wondering I watched;
Nor could the secular fairy ever change
My wonder into curiosity.
All my emotion and imagining

[1] From D.'s second series of *Fleet Street Eclogues* (1896). The speaker is Ninian, whose experiences parallel D.'s own.

Were of the finest tissue that is woven
From sense and thought. No well-thumbed page appeared
In the hard book of memory when I woke:
Amazed I trembled newly into life:
I seemed to be created every morn.
A golden trumpet pealed along the sky:
The sun arose; the whole earth rushed upon me.
Sometimes the tree that stroked my window-pane
Was more than I could grasp; sometimes my thought
Absorbed the universe, which fell away
And dwindled from my ken, as if my mind
Had been the roomy continent of space.—
My way of life led me to London town,
And difficulties—which I overcame,
Equipped with patience and necessity.
Then suddenly before my thoughts might leap
Resurgent from the living tomb of care
And dip their wings in dawn, about me clung
The slimy folds of sin: its nether coils
Are hidden in the sepulchre of time,
The glutted past; the pallid future strains
In travail with its fiery eyes and fangs:
I peer from out the slippery middle wreaths
And see blurred visions of the world, or watch
The flashing scenes that haunt my memory.

22
The Last Rose[1]

'Oh, which is the last rose?'
A blossom of no name.
At midnight the snow came;
At daybreak a vast rose,
In darkness unfurled,
O'er-petaled the world.

Its odourless pallor,
Blossomed forlorn,
Till radiant valour
Established the morn—
Till the night
Was undone
In her fight
With the sun.

The brave orb in state rose
And crimson he shone first;
While from the high vine
Of heaven the dawn burst,
Staining the great rose
From sky-line to sky-line.
The red rose of morn
A white rose at noon turned;
But at sunset reborn,
All red again soon burned.
Then the pale rose of noonday
Re-bloomed in the night
And spectrally white
In the light
Of the moon lay.

But the vast rose
Was scentless,

[1] This appeared in the *Speaker*, 12 (30 Nov. 1895), 594, and in *The Last Ballad.*

And this is the reason:
When the blast rose
Relentless,
And brought in due season
The snow-rose, the last rose
Congealed in its breath,
There came with it treason;
The traitor was Death.

In lee-valleys crowded,
The sheep and the birds
Were frozen and shrouded
In flights and in herds.
In highways
And byways
The young and the old
Were tortured and maddened
And killed by the cold.
But many were gladdened
By the beautiful last rose,
The blossom of no name
That came when the snow came,
In darkness unfurled—
The beautiful vast rose
That filled all the world.

23

A Woman and her Son[1]

'Has he come yet?' the dying woman asked.
'No,' said the nurse. 'Be quiet.'

'When he comes
Bring him to me: I may not live an hour.'

'Not if you talk. Be quiet.'

'When he comes
Bring him to me.'

'Hush, will you!'

Night came down.
The cries of children playing in the street
Suddenly rose more voluble and shrill;
Ceased, and broke out again; and ceased and broke
In eager prate; then dwindled and expired.

'Across the dreary common once I saw
The moon rise out of London like a ghost.
Has the moon risen? Is he come?'

'Not yet.
Be still, or you will die before he comes.'

The working-men with heavy iron tread,
The thin-shod clerks, the shopmen neat and plump
Home from the city came. On muddy beer
The melancholy mean suburban street
Grew maudlin for an hour; pianos waked
In dissonance from dreams of rusty peace,

[1] Written in 1896, shortly before D.'s own mother's death in Edinburgh in September that year. D. worked on the proofs of *New Ballads*, in which the poem appeared, on the eve of the funeral.

And unpitched voices quavered tedious songs
Of sentiment infirm or nerveless mirth.

'Has he come yet?'

'Be still or you will die!'

And when the hour of gaiety had passed,
And the poor revellers were gone to bed,
The moon among the chimneys wandering long
Escaped at last, and sadly overlooked
The waste raw land where doleful suburbs thrive.

Then came a firm quick step—measured but quick;
And then a triple knock that shook the house
And brought the plaster down.

'My son!' she cried.

'Bring him to me!'

He came; the nurse went out.

'Mother, I thought to spare myself this pain,'
He said at once, 'but that was cowardly.
And so I come to bid you try to think,
To understand at last.'

'Still hard, my son?'

'Hard as nether millstone.'

'But I hope
To soften you,' she said, 'before I die.'

'And I to see you harden with a hiss
As life goes out in the cold bath of death.
Oh, surely now your creed will set you free
For one great moment, and the universe
Flash on your intellect as power, power, power,
Knowing not good or evil, God or sin,

But only everlasting yea and nay.
Is weakness greatness? No, a thousand times!
Is force the greatest? Yes, for ever yes!
Be strong, be great, now you have come to die.'

'My son you seem to me a kind of prig.'

'How can I get it said? Think, mother, think!
Look back upon your fifty wretched years
And show me anywhere the hand of God.
Your husband saving souls—O, paltry souls
That need salvation!—lost the grip of things,
And left you penniless with none to aid
But me the prodigal. Back to the start!
An orphan girl, hurt, melancholy, frail,
Before you learned to play, your toil began:
That might have been your making, had the weight
Of drudgery, the unsheathed fire of woe
Borne down and beat on your defenceless life:
Souls shrivel up in these extremes of pain,
Or issue diamonds to engrave the world;
But yours before it could be made or marred,
Plucked from the burning, saved by faith, became
Inferior as a thing of paste that hopes
To pass for real in heaven's enduing light.
You married then a crude evangelist,
Whose soul was like a wafer that can take
One single impress only.'

'Oh, my son!
Your father!'

'He, my father! These are times
When all must to the crucible—no thought,
Practice, or use, or custom sacro-sanct
But shall be violable now. And first
If ever we evade the wonted round,
The stagnant vortex of the eddying years,
The child must take the father by the beard,
And say, "What did you in begetting me?"'

'I will not listen!'

'But you shall, you must—
You cannot help yourself. Death in your eyes
And voice, and I to torture you with truth,
Even as your preachers for a thousand years
Pestered with falsehood souls of dying folk.
Look at the man, your husband. Of the soil;
Broad, strong, adust;[2] head, massive; eyes of steel;
Yet some way ailing, for he understood
But one idea, and he married you.'

The dying woman sat up straight in bed;
A ghastly blush glowed on her yellow cheek,
And flame broke from her eyes, but words came not.

The son's pent wrath burnt on. 'He married you;
You were his wife, his servant; cheerfully
You bore him children; and your house was hell.
Unwell, half-starved, and clad in cast-off clothes,
We had no room, no sport; nothing but fear
Of our evangelist, whose little purse
Opened to all save us; who squandered smiles
On wily proselytes, and gloomed at home.
You had eight children; only three grew up:
Of these, one died bedrid, and one insane,
And I alone am left you. Think of it!
It matters nothing if a fish, a plant
Teem with waste offspring, but a conscious womb!
Eight times you bore a child, and in fierce throes,
For you were frail and small: of all your love,
Your hopes, your passion, not a memory steals
To smooth your dying pillow, only I
Am here to rack you. Where does God appear?'

'God shall appear,' the dying woman said.
'God has appeared; my heart is in his hand.
Were there no God, no Heaven!—Oh, foolish boy!

[2] *adust*: gloomy in features and temperament (obsolete).

You foolish fellow! Pain and trouble here
Are God's benignest providence—the whip
And spur to Heaven. But joy was mine below—
I am unjust to God—great joy was mine:
Which makes Heaven sweeter too; because if earth
Afford such pleasure in mortality
What must immortal happiness be like!
Eight times I was a mother. Frail and small?
Yes, but the passionate, courageous mate
Of a strong man. Oh, boy! You paltry boy!
Hush! Think! Think—you! Eight times I bore a child,
Eight souls for God! In Heaven they wait for me—
My husband and the seven. I see them all!
And two are children still—my little ones!
While I have sorrowed here, shrinking sometimes
From that which was decreed, my Father, God,
Was storing Heaven with treasure for me. Hush!
My dowry in the skies! God's thoughtfulness!
I see it all! Lest Heaven might, unalloyed,
Distress my shy soul, I leave earth in doubt
Of your salvation: something to hope and fear
Until I get accustomed to the peace
That passeth understanding. When you come—
For you will come, my son . . .'

Her strength gave out;
She sank down panting, bathed in tears and sweat.

'Could I but touch your intellect,' he cried,
'Before you die! Mother, the world is mad:
This castle in the air, this Heaven of yours,
Is the lewd dream of morbid vanity.
For each of us death is the end of all;
And when the sun goes out the race of men
Shall cease for ever. It is ours to make
This farce of fate a splendid tragedy:
Since we must be the sport of circumstance,
We should be sportsmen, and produce a breed
Of gallant creatures, conscious of their doom,
Marching with lofty brows, game to the last.
Oh good and evil, heaven and hell are lies!

But strength is great: there is no other truth:
This is the yea-and-nay that makes men hard.
Mother, be hard and happy in your death.'

'What do you say? I hear the waters roll . . .'
Then, with a faint cry, striving to arise—
'After I die I shall come back to you,
And then you must believe; you must believe,
For I shall bring you news of God and Heaven!'

He set his teeth, and saw his mother die.
Outside a city-reveller's tipsy tread
Severed the silence with a jagged rent;
The tall lamps flickered through the sombre street,
With yellow light hiding the stainless stars:
In the next house a child awoke and cried;
Far off a clank and clash of shunting trains
Broke out and ceased, as if the fettered world
Started and shook its irons in the night;
Across the dreary common citywards,
The moon, among the chimneys sunk again,
Cast on the clouds a shade of smoky pearl.

And when her funeral day had come, her son,
Before they fastened down the coffin lid,
Shut himself in the chamber, there to gaze
Upon her dead face, hardening his heart.
But as he gazed, into the smooth wan cheek
Life with its wrinkles shot again; the eyes
Burst open, and the bony fingers clutched
The coffin sides; the woman raised herself,
And owl-like in her shroud blinked on the light.

'Mother, what news of God and Heaven?' he asked.

Feeble and strange, her voice came from afar:
'I am not dead: I must have been asleep.'

'Do not imagine that. You lay here dead—
Three days and nights, a corpse. Life has come back:
Often it does, although faint-hearted folk

Fear to admit it: none of those who die,
And come to life again, can ever tell
Of any bourne from which they have returned:
Therefore they were not dead, your casuists say.
The ancient jugglery that tricks the world!
You lay here dead, three days and nights. What news?
"After I die I shall come back to you,
And then you must believe"—these were your words—
"For I shall bring you news of God and Heaven."'
She cast a look forlorn about the room:
The door was shut; the worn venetian, down;
And stuffy sunlight through the dusty slats
Spotted the floor, and smeared the faded walls.
He with his strident voice and eyes of steel
Stood by relentless.

'I remember, dear,'
She whispered, 'very little. When I died
I saw my children dimly bending down
The little ones in front, to beckon me,
A moment in the dark; and that is all.'

'That was before you died—the last attempt
Of fancy to create the heart's desire.
Now mother, be courageous, now, be hard.'

'What must I say or do, my dearest son?
Oh me, the deep discomfort of my mind!
Come to me, hold me, help me to be brave,
And I shall make you happy if I can,
For I have none but you—none anywhere . . .
Mary, the youngest, whom you never saw
Looked out of Heaven first: her little hands . . .
Three days and nights, dead, and no memory! . . .
A poor old creature dying a second death,
I understand the settled treachery,
The plot of love and hope against the world.
Fearless, I gave myself at nature's call;
And when they died, my children, one by one,
All sweetly in my heart I buried them.

Who stole them while I slept? Where are they all?
My heart is eerie,[3] like a rifled grave
Where silent spiders spin among the dust,
And the wind moans and laughs under its breath.
But in a drawer . . . What is there in the drawer?
No pressure of a little rosy hand
Upon a faded cheek—nor anywhere
The seven fair stars I made. Oh love the cheat!
And hope, the radiant devil pointing up,
Lest men should cease to give the couple sport
And end the world at once! For three days dead—
Here in my coffin; and no memory!
Oh, it is hard! But I—I, too, am hard . . .
Be hard, my son, and steep your heart of flesh
In stony waters till it grows a stone,
Or love and hope will hack it with blunt knives
As long as it can feel.'

He, holding her,
With sobs and laughter spoke: his mind had snapped
Like a frayed string o'erstretched: 'Mother, rejoice;
For I shall make you glad. There is no heaven.
Your children are resolved to dust and dew:
But, mother, I am God. I shall create
The heaven of your desires. There must be heaven
For mothers and their babes. Let heaven be now!'

They found him conjuring chaos with mad words
And brandished hands across his mother's corpse.

Thus did he see her harden with a hiss
As life went out in the cold bath of death;
Thus did she soften him before she died:
For both were bigots—fateful souls that plague
The gentle world.

[3] *eerie*: afraid (Scots).

24
Waiting[1]

Within unfriendly walls
  We starve—or starve by stealth.
Oxen fatten in their stalls;
  You guard the harrier's health:
They never can be criminals,
  And can't compete for wealth.
    From the mansion and the palace
      Is there any help or hail
    For the tenants of the alleys,
      Of the workhouse and the jail?

Though lands await our toil,
  And earth half-empty rolls,
Cumberers of English soil,
  We cringe for orts[2] and doles—
Prosperity's accustomed foil,
  Millions of useless souls.
    In the gutters and the ditches
      Human vermin festering lurk—
    We, the rust upon your riches;
      We, the flaw in all your work.

Come down from where you sit;
  We look to you for aid.
Take us from the miry pit,
  And lead us undismayed:
Say, 'Even you, outcast, unfit,
  Forward with sword and spade!'
    And myriads of us idle
      Would thank you through our tears,
    Though you drove us with a bridle,
      And a whip about our ears!

[1] This appeared in the *Chap-Book* (15 Jan. 1897), 206, with the subtitle 'A Song of the Submerged Tenth'. D. dropped the subtitle when it appeared in *The Last Ballad*.

[2] *orts*: scraps of food left over after a meal.

From cloudy cape to cape
   The teeming waters seethe;
Golden grain and purple grape
   The regions overwreathe.
Will no one help us to escape?
   We scarce have room to breathe.
      You might try to understand us:
         We are waiting night and day
      For a captain to command us,
         And the word we must obey.

25

Earth to Earth[1]

Where the region grows without a lord,
  Between the thickets emerald-stoled,
In the woodland bottom the virgin sward,
  The cream of the earth, through depths of mold
    O'erflowing wells from secret cells,
While the moon and the sun keep watch and ward,
  And the ancient world is never old.

Here, alone, by the grass-green hearth
  Tarry a little: the mood will come!
Feel your body a part of earth;
  Rest and quicken your thought at home;
    Take your ease with the brooding trees;
Join in their deep-down silent mirth
  The crumbling rock and the fertile loam.

Listen and watch! The wind will sing;
  And the day go out by the western gate;
The night come up on her darkling wing;
  And the stars with flaming torches wait.
    Listen and see! And love and be
The day and the night and the world-wide thing
  Of strength and hope you contemplate.

No lofty Patron of Nature! No;
  Nor a callous devotee of Art!
But the friend and the mate of the high and the low,
  And the pal to take the vermin's part,
    Your inmost thought divinely wrought,
In the grey earth of your brain aglow
  With the red earth burning in your heart.

[1] This appeared in the *Speaker*, 16 (27 Nov. 1897), 604, and in *The Last Ballad*.

26
Insomnia[1]

He wakened quivering on a golden rack
  Inlaid with gems: no sign of change, no fear
  Or hope of death came near;
Only the empty ether hovered black
  And about him stretched upon his living bier,
Of old by Merlin's Master deftly wrought:
  Two Seraphim of Gabriel's helpful race
  In that far nook of space
With iron levers wrenched and held him taut.

The Seraph at his head was Agony;
  Delight, more terrible, stood at his feet:
  Their sixfold pinions beat
The darkness, or were spread immovably
  Poising the rack, whose jewelled fabric meet
To strain a god, did fitfully unmask
  With olive light of chrysoprases dim
  The smiling Seraphim
Implacably intent upon their task.

27
The Gift[2]

Solacing tears,
  The suppliant's sigh,
Repentant years
  The fates deny;
But tortured breath
  Has one ally,
The gift of death,
  The power to die.

[1] First published in the *Saturday Review*, 85 (4 June 1898), 745, with a companion poem, 'Morning', under the general title 'Not Otherwise'. It appeared in *The Last Ballad*.

[2] Written in 1897 or 1898 at Shoreham, where D. went to recover from a breakdown in health. It appeared in *The Last Ballad*.

28
The Price[1]

Terrible is the price
  Of beginning anew, of birth;
For Death has loaded dice.

Men hurry and hide like mice;
  But they cannot evade the Earth,
And Life, Death's fancy price.

A blossom once or twice,
  Love lights on Summer's hearth;
But Winter loads the dice.

In jangling shackles of ice,
  Ragged and bleeding, Mirth
Pays the Piper's price.

The dance is done in a trice:
  Death belts his bony girth;
And struts, and rattles his dice.

Let Virtue play or Vice,
  Beside his sombre firth
Life is the lowest price
Death wins with loaded dice.

[1] Written at Shoreham, probably in 1898. It appeared in *The Last Ballad.*

29

Eclogue: Votary and Artist[1]

VOTARY

What gloomy outland region have I won?

ARTIST

This is the Vale of Hinnom.[2] What are you?

VOTARY

A Votary of Life. I thought this tract,
With rubbish choked, had been a thoroughfare
For many a decade now.

ARTIST

No highway here!
And those who enter never can return.

VOTARY

But since my coming is an accident—

ARTIST

All who inhabit Hinnom enter there
By accident, carelessly cast aside,
Or self-inducted in an evil hour.

VOTARY

But I shall walk about it and go forth.

ARTIST

I said so when I came; but I am here.

VOTARY

What brought you hither?

ARTIST

Chance, no other power:
My tragedy is common to my kind.—
Once from a mountain-top at dawn I saw

[1] Published in the *Saturday Review*, 86 (26 Nov. 1898), 696, and as 'Eclogues III' in *The Last Ballad.* It appeared subsequently as 'Epilogue to Fleet Street Eclogues' in the *Selected Poems* of 1905.

[2] Place where human sacrifice took place and filth was burnt (biblical).

My life pass by, a pageant of the age,
Enchanting many minds with sound and light,
Array and colour, deed, device and spell.
And to myself I said aloud, 'When thought
And passion shall be rooted deep, and fleshed
In all experience man may dare, yet front
His own interrogation unabashed:
Winged also, and inspired to cleave with might
Abysses and the loftiest firmament:
When my capacity and art are ranked
Among the powers of nature, and the world
Awaits my message, I will paint a scene
Of life and death, so tender, so humane,
That lust and avarice lulled awhile, shall gaze
With open countenances; broken hearts,
The haunt, the shrine, the wailing-place of woe,
Be comforted with respite unforeseen,
And immortality reprieve despair.'
The vision beckoned me; the prophecy,
That smokes and thunders in the blood of youth,
Compelled unending effort, treacherous
Decoys of doom although these tokens were.
Across the wisdom and the wasted love
Of some who barred the way my pageant stepped:
'Thus are all triumphs paved', I said; but soon,
Entangled in the tumult of the times,
Sundered and wrecked, it ceased to pace my thought,
Wherein alone its airy nature strode;
While the smooth world, whose lord I deemed myself,
Unsheathed its claws and blindly struck me down,
Mangled my soul for sport, and cast me out
Alive in Hinnom where human offal rots,
And fires are heaped against the tainted air.

VOTARY

Escape!

ARTIST

I tried, as you will try; and then
Dauntless, I cried, 'At midnight, darkly lit
By drifts of flame whose ruddy varnish dyes

The skulls and rounded knuckles light selects
Flickering upon the refuse of despair,
Here, as it should the costly pageant ends;
And here with my last strength, since I am I,
Here will I paint my scene of life and death:
Not that I dreamt of when the eager dawn,
And inexperience, stubborn parasite
Of youth and manhood, flattered in myself
And in a well-pleased following, vanities
Of hope, belief, good-will, the embroidered stuff
That masks the cruel eyes of destiny;
But a new scene profound and terrible
As Truth, the implacable antagonist.
And yet most tender, burning, bitter-sweet
As are the briny tears and crimson drops
Of human anguish, inconsolable
Throughout all time, and wept in every age
By open wounds and cureless, such as I,
Whence issues nakedly the heart of life.'

VOTARY

What canvas and what colour could you find
To paint in Hinnom so intense a scene?

ARTIST

I found and laid no colour. Look about!
On the flame-roughened darkness whet your eyes.
This needs no deeper hue; this is the thing:
Millions of people huddled out of sight,
The offal of the world.

VOTARY

I see them now,
In groups, in multitudes, in hordes, and some
Companionless, ill-lit by tarnished fire
Under the towering darkness ceiled with smoke;
Erect, supine, kneeling or prone, but all
Sick-hearted and aghast among the bones.

ARTIST

Here pine the subtle souls that had no root,
No home below, until disease or shame

Undid the once-so-certain destiny
Imagined for the Brocken-sprite[3] of self,
While earth, which seemed a pleasant inn of dreams,
Unveiled a tedious death-bed and a grave.

VOTARY

I see! The disillusioned geniuses
Who fain would make the world sit up, by Heaven!
And dig God in the ribs, and who refuse
Their own experience: would-bes, theorists,
Artistic natures, failed reformers, knaves
And fools incompetent or overbold,
Broken evangelists and debauchees,
Inebriates, criminals, cowards, virtual slaves.

ARTIST

The world is old; and countless strains of blood
Are now effete; these loathsome ruined lives
Are innocent—if life itself be good.
Inebriate, coward, artist, criminal—
The nicknames unintelligence expels
Remorse with when the conscience hints that all
Are guilty of the misery of one.
Look at these women: broken chalices,
Whose true aroma of the spring is split
In thankless streets and with the sewage blent.

VOTARY

Harlots, you mean; the scavengers of love,
Who sweep lust from our thresholds—needful brooms
In every age; the very bolts indeed
That clench and rivet solidarity.
All this is as it has been and shall be:
I see it, note it, and go hence. Farewell.

ARTIST

Here I await you.

VOTARY

There is no way out.

[3] Spirit at Walpurgis-night revels.

ARTIST

But we are many. What? So pinched and pale
At once! Weep, and take courage. This is best,
Because the alternative is not to be.

VOTARY

But I am nothing yet, have made no mark
Upon my time; and, worse than nothing now,
Must wither in a nauseous heap of tares.[4]
Why am I outcast who so loved the world?
How did I reach this place? Hush! Let me think.
I said—what did I say and do? Nothing to mourn.
I trusted life, and life has led me here.

ARTIST

Where dull endurance only can avail.
Scarcely a tithe of men escape this fate;
And not a tithe of those who suffer know
Their utter misery.

VOTARY

And must this be
Now and for ever, and has it always been?

ARTIST

Worse now than ever and ever growing worse.
Men as they multiply use up mankind
In greater masses and in subtler ways:
Ever more opportunity, more power
For intellect, the proper minister
Of life, that will usurp authority,
With lightning at its beck and prisoned clouds.
I mean that electricity and steam
Have set a barbarous fence about the earth,
And made the oceans and the continents
Preserved estates of crafty gather-alls;
Have loaded labour with a shotted chain,
And raised the primal curse a thousand powers.

[4] *tares*: weeds among corn.

VOTARY

What? Are there honest labourers outcast here?
Dreamers, pococurantes, wanton bloods
In plenty and to spare; but surely work
Attains another goal than Hinnom!

ARTIST

Look!
Seared by the sun and carved by cold or blanched
In darkness; gnarled and twisted all awry
By rotting fogs; lamed, limb-lopped, cankered, burst,
The outworn workers!

VOTARY

I take courage then!
Since workers here abound it must be right
That men should end in Hinnom.

ARTIST

Right! How right?
The fable of the world till now records
Only the waste of life: the conquerors,
Tyrants and oligarchs, and men of ease,
Among the myriad nations, peoples, tribes,
Need not be thought of: earth's inhabitants,
Man, ape, dinornis[5] for a moment breathe,
In misery die, and to oblivion
Are dedicated all. Consider still
The circumstance that most appeals to men:
Eternal siege and ravage of the source
Of being, of beauty, and of all delight,
The hell of whoredom. God! The hourly waste
Of women in the world since time began!

VOTARY

I think of it.

ARTIST

And of the waste of men
In war—pitiful soldiers, battle-harlots.

[5] *dinornis*: flightless ostrich-sized bird of New Zealand, now extinct.

VOTARY

That also I consider.

ARTIST

Weaklings, fools
In millions who must end disastrously;
The willing hands and hearts, in millions too,
Paid with perdition for a life of toil;
The blood of women, a constant sacrifice,
Staining the streets and every altar-step;
The blood of men poured out in endless wars;
No hope, no help; the task, the stripes, the woe
Augmenting with the ages. Right, you say!

VOTARY

Do you remember how the moon appears
Illumining the night?

ARTIST

What has the moon
To do with Hinnom?

VOTARY

Call the moon to mind.
Can you? Or have you quite forgotten all
The magic of her beams?

ARTIST

Oh no! The moon
Is the last memory of ample thought,
Of joy and loveliness that one forgets
In this abode. Since first the tide of life
Began to ebb and flow in human veins,
The targe of lovers' looks, their brimming fount
Of dreams and chalice of their sighs; with peace
And deathless legend clad and crowned, the moon!

VOTARY

But I adore it with a newer love,
Because it is the offal of the globe.
When from the central nebula our orb,
Outflung, set forth upon its way through space,
Still towards its origin compelled to lean

And grope in molten tides, a belt of fire,
Home-sick, burst off at last, and towards the sun
Whirling, far short of its ambition fell,
Insphered a little distance from the earth
There to bethink itself and wax and wane,
The moon!

ARTIST

I see! I know! You mean that you
And I, and foiled ambitions every one
In every age; the outworn labourers,
Pearls of the sewer, idlers, armies, scroyles,[6]
The offal of the world, will somehow be—
Are now a lamp by night, although we deem
Ourselves disgraced, forlorn; even as the moon,
The scum and slag of earth, that, if it feels,
Feels only sterile pain, gladdens the mountains
And the spacious sea.

VOTARY

I mean it. And I mean
That the deep thoughts of immortality
And of our alienage, inventing gods
And paradise and wonders manifold,
Are rooted in the centre. We are fire,
Cut off and cooled a while: and shall return,
The earth and all thereon that live and die,
To be again candescent in the sun,
Or in the sun's intenser, purer source.
What matters Hinnom for an hour or two?
Arise and let us sing; and, singing build
A tabernacle even with these ghastly bones.

[6] *scroyles*: wretches or scoundrels.

30
The Outcast[1]

Soul, be your own
  Pleasance and mart,
A land unknown,
  A state apart.

Scowl, and be rude
  Should love entice;
Call gratitude
  The costliest vice.

Deride the ill
  By fortune sent;
Be scornful still
  If foes repent.

When curse and stone
  Are hissed and hurled,
Aloof, alone
  Disdain the world.

Soul, disregard
  The bad, the good;
Be haughty, hard,
  Misunderstood.

Be neutral; spare
  No humblest lie,
And overbear
  Authority.

Laugh wisdom down;
  Abandon fate;

[1] Andrew Turnbull in *The Poems of John Davidson* (Edinburgh, 1973) cites Emerson's essay 'Self-Reliance' as the possible inspiration for this poem. D. may have used *Selected Writings of Ralph Waldo Emerson* (London, 1888). The poem reflects D.'s mood at the time of his recovery at Shoreham. It appeared in *The Last Ballad.*

Shame the renown
  Of all the great.

Dethrone the past;
  Deed, vision—naught
Avails at last
  Save your own thought.

Though on all hands
  The powers unsheathe
Their lightning-brands
  And from beneath,

And from above
  One curse be hurled
With scorn, with love
  Affront the world.

31

From The Testaments (1901–1904)
From I. The Testament of a Vivisector[1]

Daily I passed a common, chapped and seamed
By weeks of headlong heat. A rotten hack,
Compunctious hideful of rheumatic joints
Larded with dung and clay, gaunt spectacle
Of ringbone, spavin, canker, shambled about,
And grazed the faded, sparse, disrelished tufts
That the sun's tongue of flame had left half-licked:
Family physician, coster, cat's-meat-man—
These, the indifferent fates who ruled his life.
The last had turned him loose to dissipate
A day or two of grace. But when he came—
The raw-faced knacker with his knuckly fists—
I ransomed Dobbin, pitying his case,
He seemed so cheerful maugre destiny.

Enfranchised in my meadow, all his hours
Were golden, till the end with autumn came,
Even while my impulse sundered husk and shell
Of habit and utility. Two days
He lay a-dying, and could not die. Endowed
With strength, affection, blood, nerve, hearing, sight;
Laden with lust of life for the behoof
Of Matter; gelded, bitted, scourged, starved, dying—
Where could the meaning of the riddle lie?

Submissively, like a somnambulist
Who solves his problem in a dream, I found
The atonement of it, and became its lord—
Lord of the riddle of the Universe,
Aware at full of Matter's stolid will

[1] In a note to the first in the series, D. wrote: 'This poem . . . and its successors, my 'Testaments', are addressed to those who are willing to place all ideas in the crucible, and who are not afraid to fathom what is subconscious in themselves and others.' Vivisection was a topic heatedly debated in the press at the time.

In me accomplishing its useless aim.
The whip's-man felt no keener ecstasy
When a fair harlot at the cart's-tail shrieked,
And rags of flesh with blood-soaked tawdry lace
Girdled her shuddering loins. No hallowed awe
That ever rapt a pale inquisitor,
Beholding pangs of stubborn heresy
A-sweat upon the rack, surpassed the fierce
Exalted anguish of my thought. I fixed
The creature, impotent and moribund,
With gag and fetter; sheared his filthy mane;
Cut a foot's length, tissue and tendon, 'twixt
His poll and festering withers, and hammered out
Three arches of his spine. In ropy bulk,
Stripped to my forceps, marrow, Matter's pith
Itself! A twitch, a needle's faint appeal
Recalled the gelding's life, supplied each stop
And register of sense with vibrant power
And made this faithful, dying, loathsome drudge,
One diapason of intensest pain,
Sublime and terrible in martyrdom.

I study pain, measure it and invent—
I and my compeers; for I hold again
That every passionate Materialist,
Who rends the living subject, soon is purged
Of vulgar tenderness in diligent
Delighted tormentry of bird and beast;
And, conscious or unconscious of his aim,
Fulfils the will of Matter, cutting out
A path to knowledge, undefiled with use
Or usufruct, by Matter's own resource,
Pain, alkahest[2] of all intelligence.
I study pain—pain only: I broach and tap
The agony of Matter, and work its will,
Detecting useless items—I and those
Who tortured fourscore solipeds to carve
A scale of feeling on the spinal cord;

[2] *alkahest*: universal solvent imagined by the alchemists.

Quilted with nails, and mangled flights of fowl,
Litters and nests of vermin happily
Throughout a year, discerning in the end
That anguished breath and breath of healthy ease
Differ in function by a jot, perhaps;
Or Pisan doctors whom the Florentine[3]
Furnished with criminals from a gentler doom
Withdrawn to undergo anatomy,
And masters who, before the world grew tame,
Enjoyed the handling in their honoured troughs
Of countless men and women alive and well.

[3] Lorenzo di Medici.

From II. The Testament of a Man Forbid[1]

Mankind has cast me out. When I became
So close a comrade of the day and night,
Of earth and of the seasons of the year,
And so submissive in my love of life
And study of the world that I unknew
The past and names renowned, religion, art,
Inventions, thoughts, and deeds, as men unknow
What good and evil fate befell their souls
Before their bodies gave them residence,
(How the old letter haunts the spirit still!
As if the soul were other than the sum
The body's powers make up—a golden coin,
Amount of so much silver, so much bronze!)
I said, rejoicing, 'Now I stand erect,
And am that which I am.' Compassionate
I watched a motley crowd beside me bent
Beneath unsteady burdens, toppling loads
Of volumes, news and lore antique, that showered
About their ears to be re-edified
On aching heads and shoulders overtasked.
Yet were these hodmen cheerful, ignorant
Of woe whose character it is to seem
Predestined and an honourable care:
They read their books, re-read, and read again;
They balanced libraries upon their polls,
And tottered through the valley almost prone,
But certain they were nobler than the beasts.
I saw besides in fields and cities hordes
Of haggard people soaked in filth and slime
Wherewith they fed the jaded earth the while
Their souls of ordure stank; automata
That served machines whose tyrannous revolt
Enthralled their lords, as if the mistletoe

[1] Based on a prose article, 'The Man Forbid', *Speaker*, 17 (5 Mar. 1898), 297–8. The phrase 'man forbid' comes from *Macbeth*, I. iii.

Displaying mournful gold and wintry pearls
On sufferance, should enchant the forest oak
To be its accident and parasite;
Wretches and monsters that were capable
Of joy and sorrow once, their bodies numbed,
Their souls deflowered, their reason disendowed
By noisome trades, or at the furnaces,
In drains and quarries and the sunless mines;
And myriads upon myriads, human still
Without redemption drudging till they died.

Aware how multitudes of those enslaved
No respite sought, but squandered leisure hours
Among the crowd whose choice or task it was
To balance libraries upon their polls,
I laughed a long low laugh with weeping strung,
A rosary of tears, to see mankind
So dauntless and so dull, and cried at last,
'Good people, honest people, cast them off
And stand erect, for few are helped by books.
What! will you die crushed under libraries?
Lo! thirty centuries of literature
Have curved your spines and overborne your brains!
Off with it—all of it! Stand up; behold
The earth; life, death, and day and night!
Think not the things that have been said of these;
But watch them and be excellent, for men
Are what they contemplate.'

They mocked me: 'Yah!
The fox who lost his tail! Though you are crazed
We have our wits about us.'

'Nay', I cried;
'There was besides an ape who lost his tail
That he might change to man. Undo the past!
The rainbow reaches Asgard[2] now no more;
Olympus stands untenanted; the dead

[2] City of the gods (Norse mythology).

Have their serene abode in earth itself,
Our womb, our nurture, and our sepulchre.
Expel the sweet imaginings, profound
Humanities and golden legends, forms
Heroic, beauties, tripping shades, embalmed
Through hallowed ages in the fragrant hearts
And generous blood of men; the climbing thoughts
Whose roots ethereal grope among the stars,
Whose passion-flowers perfume eternity,
Weed out and tear, scatter and tread them down;
Dismantle and dilapidate high heaven.
It has been said: Ye must be born again.
I say to you: Men must be that they are.'

. . . .

So I went forth for evermore forbid
The company of men. The Universe,
Systems and suns and all that breathes and is,
Appeared at first in that dread solitude
Only the momentary, insolent
Irruption of a glittering fantasy
Into the silent, empty Infinite.
But eyes and ears were given to me again:
With these a man may do; with these, endure.

I haunt the hills that overlook the sea.
Here in the Winter like a meshwork shroud
The sifted snow reveals the perished land,
And powders wisps of knotgrass dank and dead
That trail like faded locks on mouldering skulls
Unearthed from shallow burial. With the Spring
The west-wind thunders through the budding hedge
That stems the furrowed steep—a sound of drums,
Of gongs and muted cymbals; yellow breasts
And brown wings whirl in gusts, fly chaffering, drop,
And surge in gusts again; in wooded coombs
The hyacinth with purple diapers
The russet beechmast, and the cowslips hoard
Their virgin gold in lucent chalices;
The sombre furze, all suddenly attired

In rich brocade, the enterprise in chief
And pageant of the season, overrides
The rolling land and girds the bosomed plain
That strips her green robe to a saffron shore
And steps into the surf where threads and scales
And arabesques of blue and emerald wave
Begin to damascene the iron sea;
While faint from upland fold and covert peal
The sheep-bell and the cuckoo's mellow chime.
Then when the sovereign light from which we came,
Of earth enamoured, bends most questioning looks,
I watch the land grow beautiful, a bride
Transfigured with desire of her great lord.
Betrothal-music of the tireless larks,
Heaven-high, heaven-wide possesses all the air,
And wreathes the shining lattice of the light
With chaplets, purple clusters, vintages
Of sound from the first fragrant breath and first
Tear-sprinkled blush of Summer to the deep
Transmuted fire, the smouldering golden moons,
The wine-stained dusk of Autumn harvest-ripe;
And I behold the period of Time,
When Memory shall devolve and Knowledge lapse
Wanting a subject, and the willing earth
Leap to the bosom of the sun to be
Pure flame once more in a new time begun:
Here, as I pace the pallid doleful hills
And serpentine declivities that creep
Unhonoured to the ocean's shifting verge,
Or where with prouder curve and greener sward,
Surmounting peacefully the restless tides,
The cliffed escarpment ends in stormclad strength.

[A Vision of Heaven] *from* III. The Testament of an Empire-Builder[1]

At once my dream achieved a lonely hill
Wherefrom I saw the ocean welter wide,
Like silver founded in a hollow mould
Whose confines were the jangling seaboard strung
With chords of pebble and the magical
Horizon's glittering brink. A vapour, twirled
Upon the potter's wheel, the earth, that shapes
For pity or applause the very clouds,
Rose like a fragile urn enveloping
The spacious air: above its rounded mouth
The firmament, a disc of amethyst,
Received and echoed back in golden showers
The lark's continual fugue. This vaporous urn,
Wherein I stood coping its hill-crowned base
Diverse of silver sea and emerald land,
Like glass annealed in water, suddenly
Upon some flaw of wind or scratch of light
Crumbled together and became a cloud
That wrapped me round. Aloft a tempest bore
The cloud and me; then whirled the cloud away,
And left me standing on the verge of Heaven.

The native air thereof flattered my cheek
With velvet wings, more sweet and delicate
Than newblown zephyrs when the barley bends
Its aigrettes to the ocean-tempered breath
Of mundane summers; or touched me and grew still
Like scented eyelids of an odalisque
Profoundly learned in love, subdued and dumb
With passion in the honied orient night.
I watched the figures of the blessëd dead

[1] The vision follows on from the Empire-Builder's first dream, in which a parliament of beasts considers man's attachment to soul and conscience as a perversion of nature. The Empire-Builder's 'Vision of Heaven' justifies his 'mandate of imperial doom'.

Who wandered in the forests, or reposed
Beside the brooks in glens of amaranth,
That shamed the rainbow and in fragrance bore
The bell from valley-lilies and the rose.

There were the great who triumphed easily,
In thought and glance, in word and deed supreme;
Also the agonists who kept their arms,
Hatred and envy, burnished bright with use,
Who in their bosoms drove intolerance home,
And let it rust, making a cankered wound
To wring their hearts with rage and wind them up,
As Eastern lovers, lest their valiant love
Should slumber but a moment, in their flesh
Ingraft a poniard for a talisman,
And so transcending wake and bleed to death.
There were the warriors, they who knew that war
Can deify disgrace, project and change
Ignoble causes into golden grounds,
Who sought their foes instinctively, as bees
With fervid song in search of honey roam,
Whose daily business was the battlefield,
Their hour of rest, the tedious interval
Between two victories, who upset the world
And deluged earth with blood; and there were those
Whose craft was silence mainly and magpie speech,
Whose apparatus of innuendo, nod,
And supercilious lightning, cabinet
Chicanery and documental gloze
Did and undid and never could get done,
But keep *them* still on top; and those whose prey
Was honesty and scruple, foolish greed
And sore necessity, who paved with souls
Of friend and foe their desolate path to wealth:
Kings, statesmen, emperors, proconsuls, popes,
Dishonest brokers, robbers, millionaires.
There, too, were those who fought the conquerors
And would not yield at all; and those who died,
Contemned and poor, but straining to the last
For power and wealth, or at their proper hands,

Refusing life because they failed to break
The world's hard heart, and for a travelling rug
Strip off its glossy hide: the fallen, the slain,
The captives, madmen, bankrupts, suicides.
Kings' mistresses in separate arbours sat,
Sedately happy to be left alone;
And harlots of the street in joyful herds
Haunted the brakes and purlieus wild of heaven.
Bevies of mothers beautiful as dawn
Went up the shadowy aisles: Queens of the earth
Who yielded willing harvest of their wombs
For dynasties Time garners proudly yet,
With simple wives who loved their spouses well
And bore their chubby brats while nature would.
I saw, besides, women renowned of old,
Devout adorers of their own delight,
Who treasured health, and trained their sensual powers
With that innate prerogative of lust
Desirous of a world of virile deed,
Which made their chamber-doors the porch of death,
Their tumbled beds to bloody biers transformed,
Implacably renewing eager youth
By slaughter of successive paramours.

All these I saw at home in Heaven. All these!
And all who challenged fate and staked their lives
To win or lose the prize they coveted,
Who took their stand upon the earth and drew
Deep virtue from the centre, helped themselves,
Desired the world and willed what Matter would.

[The Tale of the Navvy],
from IV. The Testament of a Prime Minister[1]

'Man is the slave of everything he makes:
This gold and silver, stamped and milled for ease
Of business, has become his sole concern:
Enough is not enough: we cannot breathe
Without it: limpid water, healthy air
Are costly luxuries, the world has fallen
So helplessly within the mean control
Of money! (How the symbol still usurps
Authority in every province, masks
The figure, drains the life of actual things!
No vampire like ideas put to use!)
This thing cannot be said; but he, the man
I call the greatest showed the Universe
The acme of despair. A navvy, all
The brute; bone, blood and brawn; brows like an ape's,
Hawk's head, sad eyes deep-sunk, mouth leonine:
The incarnation of the will to live,
An instinct absolute. At twenty years
With pick and shovel none could touch his skill,
None face him hand to hand, none eat and drink
With appetite so ravenous, so staunch,
Such malt-proof brains; more glibly lewd in speech
Than creatures of debauch all gone to sex,
But virginal in fancy and in deed.
One evening in his twentieth year he sat
Beneath a hawthorn in a bottom-glade
That fringed the northern suburb where he lived.
Upon its tranquil shadow every tree
In golden light stood up, an emerald dome;
A vagrant wind that idled through the world,
Fingering the lucent foliage wantonly,

[1] Told to the Prime Minister by one of a group of vagabonds he meets while wandering in despair by the Thames, after he has broken down during a materialist speech to Parliament.

About the quaint suburban valley trailed
The scalloped oak-leaves, bronzed and fallen long,
That caught its rustling mantle as it passed.
Trees with their wrinkled hides, their many-ringed
Compacted boles, their heavy creaking boughs,
Their myriad leaves, the green turf thick and sweet,
Cream of the earth uprisen through fathomed depths
Of soil and sap: remembrances of these
Our natal house and only rafters once,
Our carpet, board and bed, a heritage
Occult in brain and blood, unguessed by him,
My man of men, begat a passionate sense
Of everlastingness; as old, as young,
As perdurable as the earth itself,
He couched him in the wood and heard and felt.
Anon the travelling music of the street
That distance can etherealize arose
Among the workmen's houses overhead.
Old vogue or new, melodious tune or harsh,
High-hammered in the village, softly stole
Adown the neighbouring valley, deep, remote,
Antique, eternal as the world-old mood
Of him that listened dreaming. Every tree
Upon its shadow stood; athwart the boughs
The wind, uncertain, sighed; the mellow tune
Like jewelled mist descended; moted shafts
Of dusky light escaped the journeying clouds
That hid the ample sun and left his beams
A deeper hue of topaz, chrysosperm[2]
To milt[3] the earth with harvest: thick as thoughts
A thunder of hoofs went by—four grazing hacks
By some unwonted shadow on the laund
Perturbed: a skirt, a glancing step, a shriek,
A ravished woman; and my man of men,
At one with nature in the ancient way,
Began his tragic course. A decade spent
In prison turned him out, insane, corrupt,

[2] *chrysosperm*: the way of making gold in alchemy; here golden or fiery seed.
[3] *milt*: impregnate.

The sheath decayed, the weapon dim and hacked,
The broken bits, the refuse of himself;
But with a purpose smouldering in the dust,
The ashes, embers, brands that had been once
A proper furnace and a glowing fire,
With perilous temper in the worn-out blade,
With wallflower on the ruins, a branch of stars
To light the outcast in the sunless pit,
And music beating in the broken heart.
He sought the ravished woman, and made her his;
For now the world to him was sex alone,
And she, the other moiety of the world:
None other; she, the woman of his deed,
His fate, the only woman he had known.
They lived beside the valley, sacro-sanct
To him by reason of his sudden crime;
For crime can hallow precincts, titles, tides,
As certainly as Calvary remains
The holiest spot on earth. Sometimes he wrought
With pick and shovel like a thing wound-up;
Sometimes in lethargy his days were sunk;
Sometimes his passion for the woman welled
Like founts of living colour, founts of fire
That steep the cloudy west in paradise.
Three years went by, a child with every year;
Then Fate abruptly gripped him by the throat,
And asked him of the deeds done in the flesh.
To feed and clothe the woman his fiercest toil
Required him still to starve himself. Four mouths
Beside his own! The hunger of his heart,
The fury of his appetite, the blood
That would ferment and flower; the toil, the pain,
The hopeless time to come for him and his!
When the third child was twelve months old, and she,
The lusty mother comelier every day,
An orchard-tree with blossom and with fruit
Sweet-scented and mature, this man of men,
Unwitting how the world shall cease to be,
And we and all our purpose, passion, power,
Dissolve like snow in fire and leave no stain,

Instinctively achieved the greatest deed
Recorded hitherto; and answered Fate
With utter arrogance. (The thing is known:
You read the trial? No; it made no noise.
That such a thing should happen in the world,
And pass from knowledge like a shallow jest!)
Midnight beat out upon suburban bells
A drowsy madrigal from tower to tower;
The potent summer moonbeams thronged the room;
And when their youngest child, asleep at last,
Released the woman virginal again—
For every birth restores virginity,
And a chaste year had filled the flower of hers—
My hero left his couch upon the floor,
Approached the bed where with her brood she lay,
And kneeling whispered in her ear. She blushed—
How deep a crimson mantling in the light
With silvery bloom like clusters of the vine!
She turned and kissed him, smiled and dove-like rose
As willing as a bride. 'Outside,' he said,
And pointed to the moon. Wondering she went
Clad in her nightdress. Splendid in the strength
Of madness . . . (What men do when Time and Fate,
The rack and torture of the world have driven
Them mad, reveals their inmost attribute;
For madness is the flowering of the heart,
The red rose of the soul) . . . So in the strength
Of madness, splendid as a god when gods
Haunted the world for love of womankind,
He caught her up and bore her to the wood.
Remembrance of their savage bridal-hour,
The decade's wasted womb, the later times
Of hunger, rapture, toil and fruitful love,
And the last year of longing unrelieved,
The fire and martyrdom of abstinence
Became a golden legend when he changed
The silent alley for the whispering glade,
The native power and beauty of the night,
Oh then the spicy odour of the earth,
The green scent of the boughs with dew refreshed,

The miracle of fantasy attained,
Of valiant passion and the wine of life
Gathered and crushed and emptied to the lees
Beneath a hawthorn on a grassy couch,
All dappled with the blossoms of the moon
That drifted earthward through the darkling tree!
For this unmannered love discounted Fate
Upon the very ground his crime had blessed,
The altar of the coming sacrifice,
And final triumph of the will to live!
Her bounteous bosom—hush!—her eager arms,
Her burning, proud, insatiable sex,
Her murmurs, molten kisses, deepdrawn sighs;
Then swift the knife across her milk-white throat,
And the red fountain gurgling in the grass!
Felicity for her; but anguish fierce
On him laid sudden hold and wrung him hard.
Anon an awful voice broke out in wrath,
A voice he knew not, from his entrails torn,
The inarticulate cry of consciousness
Caught in the wide toils of the Universe,
Of instant mystery suddenly aware,
Yet fronting with a deed of loudest note
The mute, Material Infinitude.
Forthwith he menaced heaven; stabbed at the moon;
Shook from his homeless eyes the flood of tears;
Girded his loins and perfected the work.
The youngest first: upon the mother's breast
He laid it softly down; at either hand
The other two: all dead—crimson and white,
A posy for the gods, sweet bloodworts culled
At midnight in a London suburb. Deep
His lonely sleep and dreamless in the house
His hands had ravaged. When the morning came
He gave himself to justice unperturbed.'

32

The World's Failure[1]

Before the mystery and the cult of sin,
Eternal sorrow and eternal toil
In old, unhallowed dens and mouldering streets,
Or model tenements and haunts of woe,
Can any hopeful thing be said or sung?

Somewhere delighted larks, forestalling day,
Ascend and garland heaven with flower and fruit,
Enwreathe and overrun the shining air,
When darkness crumbles from the firmament,
With fresco, fantasy and arabesque
Of splendid sound; but here the iron heavens
Ring to the factory-whistle, here the dawn,
All overgrown and quenched in creeping smoke,
Decays unseen. Here each promoter's face,
Employer's, owner's, broker's, merchant's, mean
As any eunuch's and as evil, tells
How souls unsexed by business come to love
Elaborate torture and the sullen joy
Of coining men and women into wealth.
But somewhere trumpets sound and gallant Knights
Fight to the death to win a lady's smile;
Somewhere a gentle voice, a tender hand
Console the anguished offal of the world;
Somewhere with breaking heart a poet sings;
Somewhere a woman loves a worthless man.

This the earth, the thing we know and hate,
The torture-chamber of the universe,
Wherein the entangled spirit, torn and shred,
And quickened to endure intenser pangs
With every pulse and interval of time,
Expects deliverance only when the sun

[1] D.'s contribution to *Wayfarer's Love: Contributions from Living Poets,* ed. Duchess of Sutherland (London, 1904), 70–1.

Reclaims our mundane fragment, to be purged
Of failure and the memory of men
In tides and tempests of millennial fire.
Yet here the nightingale throughout the night
Will sing enraptured, while the beating stars
Attend; and here a boy and girl will watch
The pallid moon with earnest looks and eyes
Of infinite appeal! Does God somewhere
Behold it all and know it to be good?

33

The Last Song[1]

'Songster'—say you?—'sing!'
  Not a note have I!
Effort cannot bring
  Fancy from the sky:
Hark!—the rusty string!
  Leave me here to die.
    'Songster, songster, sing!
      Tune your harp and try.
    Sing! we bid you sing
      Once before you die!'

Withered, angry, mad,
  Who would list to me,
Since my singing sad
  Troubled earth and sea
When my heart was glad
  And my fancy free?
    'Sad or joyful, sing!
      Look about, above!
    Trust the world and sing
      Once again of love!'

Love? I know the word:
  Love is of the rose.
Have you seen or heard
  Love among the snows?
Yet my heart is stirred!
  Nay, my fancy glows!
    'Summon all your powers;
      Sing of joy and woe—
    Love among the flowers,
      Love amidst the snow.'

[1] Written in 1905, when D. was surprised by the return of the lyric impulse after writing his Testaments. It appeared in *Holiday, and Other Poems.*

Death is but a trance:
  Life, but now begun!
Welcome change and chance:
  Though my days are done,
Let the planets dance
  Lightly round the sun!
    Morn and evening clasp
      Earth with loving hands—
    In a ruddy grasp
      All the pleasant lands!

Now I hear the deep
  Bourdon of the bee,
Like a sound asleep
  Wandering o'er the lea;
While the song-birds keep
  Urging nature's plea.
    Hark! the violets pray
      Swooning in the sun!
    Hush! the roses say
      Love and death are one!

Loud my dying rhyme
  Like a trumpet rings;
Love in death sublime
  Soars on sovran wings,
While the world and time
  Fade like shadowy things.
    'Love upon his lip
      Hovers loath to part;
    Death's benignant grip
      Fastens on his heart.'

Look, a victor hies
  Bloody from the fight,
And a woman's eyes
  Greet him in the night—
Softly from the skies
  Like sidereal light!

'Love is all in all,
  Life and death are great.
Bring a purple pall;
  Bury him in state.'

34

A Runnable Stag[1]

When the pods went pop on the broom, green broom,
  And apples began to be golden-skinned,
We harboured a stag in the Priory coomb,
  And we feathered his trail up-wind, up-wind,
  We feathered his trail up-wind—
    A stag of warrant, a stag, a stag,
    A runnable stag, a kingly crop,
    Brow, bay and tray and three on top,
    A stag, a runnable stag.

Then the huntsman's horn rang yap, yap, yap,
  And 'Forwards' we heard the harbourer shout;
But 'twas only a brocket that broke a gap
  In the beechen underwood, driven out,
  From the underwood antlered out
    By warrant and might of the stag, the stag,
    The runnable stag, whose lordly mind
    Was bent on sleep, though beamed and tined
    He stood, a runnable stag.

So we tufted the covert till afternoon
  With Tinkerman's Pup and Bell-of-the-North;
And hunters were sulky and hounds out of tune
  Before we tufted the right stag forth,
  Before we tufted him forth,
    The stag of warrant, the wily stag,
    The runnable stag with his kingly crop,
    Brow, bay and tray and three on top,
    The royal and runnable stag.

It was Bell-of-the-North and Tinkerman's Pup
  That stuck to the scent till the copse was drawn.

[1] Inspired by Richard Jefferies's *Red Deer* (London, 1894). Andrew Turnbull, in *The Poems of John Davidson* (Edinburgh, 1973), 498, suggests G. Whyte-Melville's *Katerfelto* (London, 1875) as another possible source. The poem appeared as 'A Ballad of a Runnable Stag' in the *Pall Mall Magazine*, 36 (July–Dec. 1905), 230–3, and later with the present title in *Holiday, and Other Poems*.

'Tally ho! tally ho!' and the hunt was up,
The tufters whipped and the pack laid on,
The resolute pack laid on,
And the stag of warrant away at last,
The runnable stag, the same, the same,
His hoofs on fire, his horns like flame,
A stag, a runnable stag.

'Let your gelding be: if you check or chide,
He stumbles at once and you're out of the hunt;
For three hundred gentlemen, able to ride,
On hunters accustomed to bear the brunt,
Accustomed to bear the brunt,
And after the runnable stag, the stag,
The runnable stag with his kingly crop,
Brow, bay and tray and three on top,
The right, the runnable stag.'

By perilous path in coomb and dell,
The heather, the rocks, and the river-bed,
The pace grew hot, for the scent lay well,
And a runnable stag goes right ahead,
The quarry went right ahead—
Ahead, ahead, and fast and far;
His antlered crest, his cloven hoof,
Brow, bay and tray and three aloof,
The stag, the runnable stag.

For a matter of twenty miles and more,
By the densest hedge and the highest wall,
Through herds of bullocks he baffled the lore
Of harbourer, huntsman, hounds and all,
Of harbourer hounds and all—
The stag of warrant, the wily stag,
For twenty miles, and five and five,
He ran, and he never was caught alive,
This stag, this runnable stag.

When he turned at bay in the leafy gloom,
In the emerald gloom where the brook ran deep,

He heard in the distance the rollers boom,
  And he saw in a vision of peaceful sleep,
  In a wonderful vision of sleep,
    A stag of warrant, a stag, a stag,
    A runnable stag in a jewelled bed,
    Under the sheltering ocean dead,
    A stag, a runnable stag.

So a fateful hope lit up his eye,
  And he opened his nostrils wide again,
And he tossed his branching antlers high
  As he headed the hunt down the Charlock glen,
  As he raced down the echoing glen
    For five miles more, the stag, the stag,
    For twenty miles, and five and five,
    Not to be caught now, dead or alive,
    The stag, the runnable stag.

Three hundred gentlemen, able to ride,
  Three hundred horses as gallant and free,
Beheld him escape on the evening tide,
  Far out till he sank in the Severn Sea,
  Till he sank in the depths of the sea—
    The stag, the buoyant stag, the stag
    That slept at last in a jewelled bed
    Under the sheltering ocean spread
    The stag, the runnable stag.

35

London Bridge[1]

Much tolerance and genial strength of mind
Unbiassed witnesses who wish to find
This railway-station possible at all
Must cheerfully expend. Artistical
Ideas wither here: a magic power
Alone can pardon and in pity dower
With fictive charm a structure so immane.[2]
How then may fancy, to begin with, feign
An origin for such a roundabout
Approach—so intricate, yet so without
Intention, and so spanned by tenebrous
And thundering viaducts? Grotesquely, thus:—
One night the disposition of the ward
Was shifted; for the streets with one accord,
Enfranchised by a landslip, danced the hay
And innocently jumbled up the way.
And so we enter. Here, without perhaps,
Except the automatic money-traps,
Inside the station, everything's so old,
So inconvenient, of such manifold
Perplexity, and, as a mole might see,
So strictly what a station shouldn't be,
That no idea minifies it crude
And yet elaborate ineptitude,
But some such fancied cataclysmal birth:—
Out of the nombles[3] of the martyred earth
This old, unhappy terminus was hurled
Back from a day of small things when the world
At twenty miles an hour still stood aghast,
And thought the penny post mutation vast,
As change itself. Before the Atlantic race
Developed turbined speed; before life's pace

[1] Based on an article, 'Automatic Augury and the Crystal Palace', *Glasgow Herald* (18 Mar. 1905), 9. It appeared as 'A Certain Railway Terminus', *Westminster Gazette* (9 Jan. 1909), 2, and in *Fleet Street, and Other Poems.*

[2] *immane*: monstrous, savage (archaic). [3] *nombles*: entrails.

Was set by automobilism; before
The furthest stars came thundering at the door
To claim close kindred with the sons of men;
Before the lettered keys outsped the pen;
Ere poverty was deemed the only crime
Or wireless news annihilated time,
Divulged now by an earthquake in the night,
This ancient terminus first saw the light.

A natural magic having gravely made
This desperate station possible, delayed
No longer by its character uncouth,
The innocent adventurer, seeking truth
Imaginative, if it may be, plays
His vision, penetrant as chemic rays,
Upon the delta wide of platforms, whence
Discharges into London's sea, immense
A turbulent, a brimming human flood,
A river inexhaustible of blood
That turns the wheels, and by a secret, old
As labour, changes heart-beats into gold
For those that toil not; all the gutters run,
Houses are daubed, with it; and moon and sun
Splashed as they spin. And yet this human tide,
As callous as the glaciers that glide
A foot a day, but as a torrent swift,
Sweeps unobservant save of time—for thrift
Or dread disposes clockwards every glance—
Right through the station which a seismic dance
Chimerical alone can harmonize
Even in imagination's friendly eyes.

Clearly a brimming tide of mind as well
As blood, whose ebb and flow is buy and sell,
Engulfed by London's storm and stress of trade
Before it reached the civic sea, and made
Oblivious, knowing nought terrestrial
Except that time is money, and money all.

Or when a portly dealer, well-to-do,
Chances to see it as he passes through,

Or boy or girl not yet entirely swamped
In ways and means and business of accompt,
About the many-platformed embouchure
And utterance of suburban life obscure
A liberal œillade[4] tosses, with a note
Chromatic, crimson van and crimson coat,
The parcel-post, and many a crimson shrine
Of merchandise mechanical combine
To reassure them as a point of war
Inspires the soldier; for the cannon's roar,
The trumpet's blast, the thunder of the drum
Ane crimson motives; and the city's hum,
The noise of battle, and a ruddy sky
May echo in the selfsame harmony.

Save when the glance of age whose brisk affairs
Look up on 'Change,[5] of youth untouched by care's
Inhibitory wand that palsies thought,
No other gracious sign appears, nor aught
Distinctly personal, innate or earned,
In the dull, rapid passage of concerned
Expression from the station to the street,
Until a dire resemblance of defeat
In one set visage hides the common face:
Such a premonstrant shadow of disgrace,
Such gray alarm, such sickening for despair
Is only seen in urban crowds, for there
The broken broker feels himself alone,
Exempt from scrutiny even of his own
Protean introspection, and as free
As genius, or as fallen spirit, to be
The very image of the thing he is—
A figure on the brink of the abyss,
The failure and the scapegoat of the mart,
The loser in the game, the tragic part,
Wherein some novice mastered by the play
Without rehearsal triumphs every day.

[4] *œillade*: look.
[5] *on 'Change*: at the exchange, i.e. the place where business is transacted.

36

The Crystal Palace[1]

Contraption,—that's the bizarre, proper slang,
Eclectic word, for this portentous toy,
The flying-machine, that gyrates stiffly, arms
A-kimbo, so to say, and baskets slung
From every elbow, skating in the air.
Irreverent, we; but Tartars from Thibet
May deem Sir Hiram[2] the Grandest Lama, deem
His volatile machinery best, and most
Magnific, rotatory engine, meant
For penitence and prayer combined, whereby
Petitioner as well as orison
Are spun about in space: a solemn rite
Before the portal of that fane unique,
Victorian temple of commercialism,
Our very own eighth wonder of the world.
The Crystal Palace.

So sublime! Like some
Immense crustacean's gannoid skeleton,
Unearthed, and cleansed, and polished! Were it so
Our paleontological respect
Would shield it from derision; but when a shed,
Intended for a palace, looks as like
The fossil of a giant myriapod! . . .
'Twas Isabey[3]—sarcastic wretch!—who told
A young aspirant, studying tandem art
And medicine, that he certainly was born

[1] Based on the prose article 'Automatic Augury and the Crystal Palace', *Glasgow Herald* (18 Mar. 1905), 9. D.'s impressions were supplemented by another visit with Max Beerbohm in June 1906 (see Letters 17 and 18). He and Beerbohm are the 'Irreverent, we' in the first stanza. The poem was first published in two parts, as 'The Crystal Palace' (ll. 1–145; ll. 282-309), and 'The Crystal Palace *à la mode* (ll. 144–281). *Westminster Gazette* (28 Nov. 1908: 3, and 23 Jan. 1909: 2, respectively).

[2] Sir Hiram Maxim (1840–1916), an American engineer famous for his development of the machine-gun.

[3] Jean Baptiste Isabey (1767–1855), French portrait-painter.

To be a surgeon: 'When you try', he said,
'To paint a boat you paint a tumour.'

No
Idea of its purpose, and no word
Can make your glass and iron beautiful.
Colossal ugliness may fascinate
If something be expressed; and time adopts
Ungainliest stone and brick and ruins them
To beauty; but a building lacking life,
A house that must not mellow or decay?—
'Tis nature's outcast. Moss and lichen? Stains
Of weather? From the first Nature said 'No!
Shine there unblessed, a witness of my scorn!
I love the ashlar and the well-baked clay;
My seasons can adorn them sumptuously:
But you shall stand rebuked till men ashamed,
Abhor you, and destroy you and repent!'

But come: here's crowd; here's mob; a gala day!
The walks are black with people: no one hastes;
They all pursue their purpose business-like—
The polo-ground, the cycle-track; but most
Invade the palace glumly once again.
It is 'again'; you feel it in the air—
Resigned habitués on every hand:
And yet agog; abandoned, yet concerned!
They can't tell why they come; they only know
They must shove through the holiday somehow.

In the main floor the fretful multitude
Circulates from the north nave to the south
Across the central transept—swish and tread
And murmur, like a seaboard's mingled sound.
About the sideshows eddies swirl and swing:
Distorting mirrors; waltzing-tops—wherein
Couples are wildly spun contrariwise
To your revolving platform; biographs,
Or rifle-ranges; panoramas: choose!

As stupid as it was last holiday?
They think so,—every whit! Outside, perhaps?

A spice of danger in the flying-machine?
A few who passed that whirligig, their hopes
On higher things, return disconsolate
To try the Tartar's volant oratory.
Others again, no more anticipant
Of any active business in their own
Diversion, joining stalwart folk who sought
At once the polo-ground, the cycle-track,
Accept the ineludible; while some
(Insidious anti-climax here) frequent
The water-entertainments—shallops, chutes
And rivers subterrene:—thus, passive, all,
Like savages bewitched, submit at last
To be the dupes of pleasure, sadly gay—
Victims, and not companions, of delight!

Not all! The garden-terrace:—hark, behold,
Music and dancing! People by themselves
Attempting happiness! A box of reeds—
Accordian, concertina, seraphine—
And practised fingers charm advertent feet!
The girls can dance; but, O their heavy-shod,
Unwieldy swains!—No matter:—hatless heads,
With hair undone, eyes shut and cheeks aglow
On blissful shoulders lie:—such solemn youths
Sustaining ravished donahs! Round they swing,
In time or out, but unashamed and all
Enchanted with the glory of the world.
And look!—Among the laurels on the lawns
Torn coats and ragged skirts, starved faces flushed
With passion and with wonder!—hid away
Avowedly; but seen—and yet not seen!
None laugh; none point; none notice: multitude
Remembers and forgives; unwisest love
Is sacrosanct upon a holiday.
Out of the slums, into the open air
Let loose for once, their scant economies
Already spent, what was there left to do?
O sweetly, tenderly, devoutly think,
Shepherd and Shepherdess in Arcady!

A heavy shower; the Palace fills; begins
The business and the office of the day,
The eating and the drinking—only real
Enjoyment to be had, they tell you straight
Now that the shifty weather fails them too.
But what's the pother here, the blank dismay?
Money has lost its value at the bars:
Like tavern-tokens when the Boar's Head rang
With laughter and the Mermaid swam in wine,
Tickets are now the only currency.
Before the buffets, metal tables packed
As closely as mosaic, with peopled chairs
Cementing them, where damsels in and out
Attend with food, like disembodied things
That traverse rock as easily as air—
These are the havens, these the happy isles!
A dozen people fight for every seat—
Without a quarrel, unturbently: O,
A peaceable, a tame, a timorous crowd!
And yet relentless: this they know they need;
Here have they money's worth—some food, some drink;
And so alone, in couples, families, groups,
Consuming and consumed—for as they munch
Their victuals all their vitals ennui gnaws—
They sit and sit, and fain would sit it out
In tedious gormandize till firework-time.
But business beats them; those who sit must eat.
Tickets are purchased at besieged Kiosks,
And when their value's spent—with such a grudge!—
They rise to buy again, and lose their seats;
For this is Mob, unhappy locust-swarm,
Instinctive, apathetic, ravenous.

Beyond a doubt a most unhappy crowd!
Some scores of thousands searching up and down
The north nave and the south nave hungrily
For space to sit and rest to eat and drink:
Or captives in a labyrinth, or herds
Imprisoned in a vast arena; here
A moment clustered; there entangled; now
In reaches sped and now in whirlpools spun

With noises like the wind and like the sea,
But silent vocally: they hate to speak:
Crowd; Mob; a blur of faces featureless,
Of forms inane; a stranded shoal of folk.

Astounding in the midst of this to meet
Voltaire, the man who worshipped first, who made
Indeed, the only god men reverence now,
Public Opinion. There he sits alert—
A cast of Houdon's[4] smiling philosophe.
Old lion-fox, old tiger-ape—what names
They gave him!—better charactered by one
Who was his heir: 'The amiable and gay'.
So said the pessimist who called life sour
And drank it to the dregs.[5] Enough: Voltaire—
About to speak: hands of a mummy clutch
The fauteuil's arms; he listens to the last
Before reply; one foot advanced; a new
Idea radiant in his wrinkled face.

Lunch in the grill-room for the well-to-do,
The spendthrifts and the connoisseurs of food—
Gourmet, gourmand, bezonian,[6] epicure.
Reserved seats at the window?—Surely; you
And I must have the best place everywhere.
A deluge smudges out the landscape. Watch
The waiters since the scenery's not on view.
A harvest-day with them, our Switzers[7]—knights
Of the napkin! How they balance loaded trays
And though they push each other spill no drop!
And how they glare at lazy lunchers, snatch
Unfinished plates sans 'by your leave', and fling
The next dish down, before the dazzled lout
(The Switzer knows his man) has time to con
The menu, every tip precisely gauged,
Precisely earned, no service thrown away.

[4] Jean Antoine Houdon (1741–1828), French sculptor.
[5] Arthur Schopenhauer (1788–1860), author of *The World as Will and Idea* (1819).
[6] *bezonian*: archaic word for 'rascal', here used to mean 'carouser', probably through an association of the word with 'bezzling'.
[7] Mercenary Swiss bodyguards.

Sign of an extra douceur, reprimand
Is welcomed, and the valetudinous
Voluptuary served devoutly: he
With cauteries on his cranium; dyed moustache;
Teeth like a sea-wolf's, each a work of art
Numbered and valued singly; copper skin;
And nether eyelids pouched:—why, he alone
Is worth a half-day's wage! Waiters for him
Are pensioners of indigestion, paid
As secret criminals disburse blackmail,
As Attic gluttons sacrificed a cock
To Æsculapius[8] to propitiate
Hygeia[9]—if the classic flourish serves!

'Grilled soles?'—for us:—Kidneys to follow.—Now,
Your sole, sir; eat it with profound respect.
A little salt with one side;—scarce a pinch!
The other side with lemon;—tenderly!
Don't crush the starred bisection;—count the drops!
Those who begin with lemon miss the true
Aroma: quicken sense with salt, and then
The subtle, poignant, citric savour tunes
The delicate texture of the foam-white fish,
Evolving palatable harmony
That music might by happy chance express.
A crust of bread—(eat slowly; thirty chews,
Gladstonian rumination)—to change the key.
And now the wine—a well-decanted, choice
Chateau, *bon per*, a decade old; not more;
A velvet claret, piously unchilled.
A boiled potato with the kidney . . . No!
Barbarian! Vandal! Sauce? 'Twould ruin all!
The kidney's the potato's sauce. Perpend:
You taste the esoteric attribute
In food; and know that all necessity
Is beauty's essence. Fill your glass: salute
The memory of the happy neolith

[8] God of medicine and healing. 'A cock to Æsculapius' means to give thanks (or pay the doctor's bill) after an illness (classical mythology).
[9] Goddess of health and daughter of Æsculapius (classical mythology).

Who had the luck to hit on roast and boiled.
Finish the claret.—Now the rain has gone
The clouds are winnowed by the sighing south,
And hidden sunbeams through a silver woof
A warp of pallid bronze in secret ply.

Cigars and coffee in the billiard-room.
No soul here save the marker, eating chops;
The waiter and the damsel at the bar,
In listless talk. A most uncanny thing,
To enter suddenly a desolate cave
Upon the margent of the sounding Mob!
A hundred thousand people, class and mass,
In and about the palace, and not a pair
To play a hundred up! The billiard-room's
The smoking-room; and spacious too, like all
The apartments of the Palace:—why
Unused on holidays? The marker: aged;
Short, broad, but of a presence; reticent
And self-respecting; not at all the type:—
'O well', says he: 'the business of the room
Fluctuates very little, year in, year out.
My customers are seasons mostly.' One
On the instant enters: a curate, very much
At ease in Zion—and in Sydenham.
He tells two funny stories—not of the room;
And talks about the stage. 'In London now',
He thinks, 'the play's the thing. He undertakes
To entertain and not to preach; you see,
It's with the theatre and the music-hall,
Actor and artiste, the parson must compete.
Every bank-holiday and special day
The Crystal Palace sees him. Yes; he feels
His hand's upon the public pulse on such
Occasions.' O, a sanguine clergyman!

Heard in the billiard-room the sound of Mob,
Occult and ominous, besets the mind:
Something gigantic, something terrible
Passes without; repasses; lingers; goes;

Returns and on the threshold pants in doubt
Whether to knock and enter, or burst the door,
In hope of treasure and a living prey.
The vainest fantasy! Rejoin the crowd:
At once the sound depreciates. Up and down
The north nave and the south nave hastily
Some tens of thousands walk, silent and sad.
A most unhappy people.—Hereabout
Cellini's[10] Perseus ought to be. Not that;
That's stucco—and Canova's:[11] a stupid thing;
The face and posture of a governess—
A nursery governess who's had the nerve
To pick a dead mouse up. It used to stand
Beside the billiard-room, against the wall,
A cast of Benvenuto's masterpiece—
That came out lame, as he foretold, despite
His dinner dishes in the foundry flung.
They shift their sculpture here haphazard.—That?
King Francis—by Clesinger;[12]—on a horse.
Absurd: most mounted statues are.—And this?
Verrochio's[13] Coleone. Not absurd:
Grotesque and strong, the battle-harlot rides
A stallion; fore and aft, his saddle, peaked
Like a mitre, grips him as in a vice.
In heavy armour mailed; his lifted helm
Reveals his dreadful look; his brows are drawn;
Four wrinkles deeply trench his muscular face;
His left arm half-extended, and the reins
Held carelessly, although the gesture's tense;
His right hand wields a sword invisible;
Remorseless pressure of his lips protrudes
His mouth; he would decapitate the world.

The light is artificial now; the place
Phantasmal like a beach in hell where souls
Are ground together by an unseen sea.

[10] Benvenuto Cellini (1500–71), Renaissance sculptor.
[11] Antonio Canova (1757–1822), Italian sculptor and painter.
[12] Jean-Baptiste Clesinger (1814–83), French sculptor.
[13] Andrea del Verrochio (1433–88), Florentine painter and sculptor.

A dense throng in the central transept, wedged
So tightly they can neither clap nor stamp,
Shouting applause at something, goad themselves
In sheer despair to think it rather fine:
'We came here to enjoy ourselves. Bravo,
Then! Are we not?' Courageous folk beneath
The brows of Michael Angelo's Moses dance
A cakewalk in the dim Renascence Court.
Three people in the silent Reading-room
Regard us darkly as we enter: three
Come in with us, stare vacantly about,
Look from the window and withdraw at once.
A drama; a balloon; a Beauty Show:—
People have seen them doubtless; but none of those
Deluded myriads walking up and down
The north nave and the south nave anxiously—
And aimlessly, so silent and so sad.

The day wears; twilight ends; the night comes down.
A ruddy targelike moon in a purple sky,
And the crowd waiting on the fireworks. Come:
Enough of Mob for one while. This way out—
Past Linacre and Chatham,[14] the second Charles,
Venus and Victory—and Sir William Jones[15]
In placid contemplation of a State!—
Down the long corridor to the district train.

[14] Thomas Linacre (1460–1524), founder of the Royal College of Physicians, and William Pitt the Elder, Earl of Chatham (1708–78).

[15] Sir William Jones (1746–94), orientalist.

37

From Fleet Street[1]

Interfluent night and day the tides of trade,
Labour and pleasure, law and crime, are sucked
From every urban quarter: through this strait
All business London pours. Amidst the boom
And thud of wheel and hoof the myriad feet
Are silent save to him who stands a while
And hearkens till his passive ear, attuned
To new discernment like an erudite
Musician's, which can follow note by note
The part of any player even in the din
And thrashing fury of the noisiest close
Orchestral, hears chromatic footsteps throb,
And tense susurrant speech of multitudes
That stride in pairs discussing ways and means,
Or reason with themselves, in single file
Advancing hardily on ruinous
Events; and should he listen long there comes
A second-hearing like the second-sight
Diviners knew, or as the runner gains
His second-breath; then phantom footsteps fall,
And muffled voices travel out of time:
Alsatians pass and Templars; stareabouts
For the new motion of Nineveh;[2] morose
Or jolly tipplers at[3] the Bolt-in-Tun,
The Devil Tavern; Johnson's[4] heavy tread
And rolling laughter; Drayton[5] trampling out
The thunder of Agincourt as up and down

[1] Based on a prose article, 'Fleet Street: A Fantasy', *Outlook* (25 Mar. 1905), 409–10, written at the request of the editor, J. L. Garvin. The poem appeared in *Fleet Street, and Other Poems.*

[2] Puppet-play in Ben Jonson's day, mentioned in *Every Man out of his Humour,* II. iii. 146–8: 'there's a new Motion of the city of Nineveh, with Jonas, and the whale, to be seen at Fleetbridge.'

[3] *at*: MS reading; 'of' in *Fleet Street, and Other Poems.*

[4] Samuel Johnson (1709–84).

[5] Michael Drayton (1563–1631), who wrote 'The Ballad of Agincourt' ('Fair Stood the Wind for France').

He paces by St. Dunstan's; Chaucer, wroth,[6]
Beating the friar that traduced the state;
And more remote, from centuries unknown,
Rumour of battle, noises of the swamp,
The gride of glacial rock, the rush of wings,
The roar of beasts that breathed a fiery air
Where fog envelops now electric light,
The music of the spheres, the humming speed
Centrifugal of molten planets loosed
From pregnant suns to find their orbits out,
The whirling spindles of the nebulæ,
The rapture of ethereal darkness strung
Illimitable in eternal space.

Fleet Street was once a silence in the ether.
The carbon, iron, copper, silicon,
Zinc, aluminium vapours, metalloids,
Constituents of the skeleton and shell
Of Fleet Street—of the woodwork, metalwork,
Brickwork, electric apparatus, drains
And printing-presses, conduits, pavement, road—
Were at the first unelemented space,
Imponderable tension in the dark
Consummate matter of eternity.
And so the flesh and blood of Fleet Street, nerve
And brain infusing life and soul, the men,
The women, woven, built and kneaded up
Of hydrogen, of azote,[7] oxygen,
Of carbon, phosphorus, chlorine, sulphur, iron,
Of calcium, kalium,[8] natrum,[9] manganese,
The warm humanities that day and night
Inhabit and employ it and inspire,
Were in the ether mingled with it, there
Distinguished nothing from the road, the shops,
The drainpipes, sewage, sweepings of the street:
Matter of infinite beauty and delight

[6] Chaucer is reputed to have been fined two shillings for beating a Franciscan Friar in Fleet Street.

[7] *azote*: gas now known as nitrogen. [8] *kalium*: potassium.

[9] *natrum*: Davidson's version of natrium i.e. sodium.

Atoning offal, filth and all offence
With soul and intellect, with love and thought;
Matter whereof the furthest stars consist,
And every interstellar wilderness
From galaxy to galaxy, the thin
Imponderable ether, matter's ghost,
But matter still, substance demonstrable
Being the icy vehicle of light.

38

Fleet Street: A Song[1]

Closes and courts and lanes,
  Devious, clustered thick,
The thoroughfare, mains and drains,
  People and mortar and brick,
Wood, metal, machinery, brains,
  Pen and composing-stick:
    Fleet Street now, but exquisite flame
      In the nebula once ere day and night
    Began their travail, or earth became,
      And all was passionate light.

Networks of wire overland,
  Conduits under the sea,
Aerial message from strand to strand
  By lightning that travels free,
Hither in haste to hand
  Tidings of destiny:
    These tingling nerves of the world's affairs
      Deliver remorseless, rendering still
    The fall of empires, the price of shares,
      The record of good and ill.

Tidal the traffic goes
  Citywards out of the town;
Townwards the evening ebb o'erflows
  The highway of old renown,
When the fog-woven curtains close,
  And the urban night comes down,
    Where souls are split and intellects spent
      O'er news vociferant near and far,
    From Hesperus hard to the Orient,
      From dawn to the evening star.

[1] This appeared in the *Pall Mall Magazine*, 40 (July–Dec. 1907), 403, as 'Fleet Street', and in *Fleet Street, and Other Poems* as 'Song'.

This the royal refrain
  That burdens the boom and the thud
Of omnibus, mobus,[2] wain,
  And the hoofs on the beaten mud,
From the Griffin at Chancery Lane
  To the portal of old King Lud[3]—
    Fleet Street, diligent night and day,
      Of news the mart and the burnished hearth,
    Seven hundred paces of narrow way,
      A notable bit of the earth.

[2] *mobus*: motor bus, with pun on 'mob'.
[3] The mythical king of Britain who gives London (Lud's town) its name.

39

The Thames Embankment[1]

As gray and dank as dust and ashes slaked
With wash of urban tides the morning lowered;
But over Chelsea Bridge the sagging sky
Had colour in it—blots of faintest bronze,
The stains of daybreak. Westward slabs of light
From vapour disentangled, sparsely glazed
The panelled firmament; but vapour held
The morning captive in the smoky east.
At lowest ebb the tide on either bank
Laid bare the fat mud of the Thames, all pinched
And scalloped thick with dwarfish surges. Cranes,
Derricks and chimney-stalks of the Surrey-side,
Inverted shadows, in the motionless,
Dull, leaden mirror of the channel hung:
Black flags of smoke broke out, and in the dead
Sheen of the water hovered underneath,
As in the upper region, listlessly.
Across the viaduct trailing plumes of steam,
The trains clanked in and out.

                                        Slowly the sun
Undid the homespun swathing of the clouds,
And splashed his image on the northern shore—
A thing extravagantly beautiful:
The glistening, close-grained canvas of the mud
Like hammered copper shone, and all about
The burning centre of the mirror'd orb's[2]
Illimitable depth of silver fire
Harmonious beams,[3] the overtones of light,
Suffused the emboss'd, metallic river bank.
Woven of rainbows a dewdrop can dissolve

[1] Based on a prose article with the same title, *Glasgow Herald* (1 Dec. 1906), 9. The poem appeared in the *Westminster Gazette* (19 Dec. 1908), 3, and in *Fleet Street, and Other Poems.*

[2] *orb's*: MS reading; 'orbs' in *Fleet Street, and Other Poems.*

[3] Comma after 'beams': *Westminster Gazette* reading.

And packed with power a simple lens can wield,
The perfect, only source of beauty, light
Reforms uncouthest shapelessness and turns
Decoloured refuse into ornament;
The leafless trees that lined the vacant street
Had all their stems picked out in golden scales,
Their branches carved in ebony; and shed
Around them by the sanction of the morn
In lieu of leaves each wore an aureole.

Barges at anchor, barges stranded, hulks
Ungainly, in the unshorn beams and rich
Replenished palette[4] of a winter sun,
Appeared ethereal, and about to glide
On high adventure chartered, swift away
For regions undiscovered.

Huddled wharfs
A while, and then once more a reach of Thames
Visibly flowing where the sun and wind
Together caught the current. Quays and piers
To Vauxhall Bridge; and there the Baltic Wharf
Exhibited its wonders: figureheads
Of the old wooden walls on gate and post—
Colossal torsos, bulky bosoms thrown
Against the storm, sublime uplifted eyes
Telling the stars. As white as ghosts
They overhung the way, usurping time
With carved memorials of the past. Forlorn
Elysium of the might of England!

Gulls,
Riparian scavengers, arose and wheeled
About my head, for morsels begging loud
With savage cries that piercingly reverbed
The tempest's dissonance. Birds in themselves
Unmusical and uninventive ape
Impressive things with mockery[5] undesigned:

[4] *palette: Westminster Gazette* reading; 'planet' in *Fleet Street, and Other Poems.*
[5] *mockery*: MS reading; 'mocking' in *Fleet Street, and Other Poems.*

The eagle's bark mimics the crashing noise
That shakes his eyry when the thunder roars;
And chanticleer's imperious trumpet-call
Re-echoes round the world his ancestor's
Barbaric high-wrought challenge to the dawn;
But birds of homely feather and tuneful throat,
With music in themselves and masterdom,
To beauty turn obsessive sights and sounds:[6]
The mounting larks, compact of joyful fire,
Render the coloured sunlight into song;
Adventurous and impassioned nightingales
Transmute the stormy equinox they breast
With courage high, for hawthorn thickets bound
When spring arrives, into the melody
That floods the forest aisles; the robin draws
Miraculously from the rippling brook
The red wine of his lay; blackbird and thrush,
Prime-artists of the woodland, proudly take
All things sonorous for their province, weave
The gold-veined thunder and the crystal showers,
The winds, the rivers and the choir of birds
In the rich strains of their chromatic score.

By magic mechanism the weltering clouds
Re-grouped themselves in continents and isles
That diapered the azure firmament;
And sombre chains of cumulus, outlined
In ruddy shade along the house-tops loomed,
Phantasmal alp on alp. The sunbeams span
Chaotic vapour into cosmic forms,
And juggled in the sky with hoods of cloud
As jesters twirl on sticks their booby-caps—
The potent sunbeams, that had fished the whole
Enormous mass of moisture from the sea,
Kneaded, divided and divided, wrought
And turned it to a thousand fantasies
Upon the ancient potter's wheel, the earth.

[6] *sights and sounds*: MS reading; 'sight and sound' in *Fleet Street, and Other Poems.*

40

From The Aristocrat of the Road[1]

. . . Through gross suburban miles
And over leagues of undistinguished ground
He plods, he tramps. Utilitarian thoughts
Of exercise and health extenuate
The dullness of the duty; he persuades
Himself he likes it; finds, where none exist,
Amazing qualities; and tires his limbs,
His thought, his fancy, o'er and o'er again.
But in the dismal watches of the night
He knows it all delusion; beauty, none,
Nor pleasure in it; ennui only—eased
By speculation on the wayside-inn,
Or country-town hotel where lunch permits
An hour's oblivion of his self-imposed,
His thriftless drudgery. Despair!—And life?
Worth picking from the gutter? No; not worth
The stooping for! Natheless,[2] a walker born,
He takes the road next day; steps out once more,
As if the world were just begun, and he,
Sole monarch; plods the suburb, tramps the waste—
Again returning baffled and dismayed.

He tries a comrade. Worse and worse!—for that,
In high pedestrianism, turns out to be
A double misery, a manacled
Contingence with vexation. Walking-tours?
Belletrists crack them up. He takes one:—lo,
A sheer atrocity! A man may like
To drink; but who would quench next morning's drouth,
Unholy though it be, with torture *forte*
Et dure in gallon draughts when by his bed
A hair gleams of the dog that bit him! Tours
Pedestrious? Madness, like the poet's who thought

[1] Based on a prose article, 'A Moribund Art', *Westminster Gazette* (8 Dec. 1906), 2–3. The poem appeared in *Fleet Street, and Other Poems.*
[2] *natheless*: nevertheless.

To write a thousand sonnets at the rate
Of three a day! And this the tale of years!

Forth from his travail and despair at last,
Crash through his plodding apparatus, breaks
The dawn of art. He recollects a mile,
Or half a mile that pleased him; a furlong here,
And there a hundred yards; or an hour's march
Over some curve of the world when everything
Above him and about him from the zenith
To the sky-edge, and radiant from his feet
Toward every cardinal point, put off the veil,
Becoming evident as guilt or love, as things
That[3] cannot hide:—becoming him,
And he becoming them; and all his past
And all his future wholly what they are,
The very form and meaning of the earth
Itself. And at these times he recollects,
And in these places, how his thoughts were clear
As crystal, deeper than the sea, as swift
As light—the pulse, the bosom and the zone
Of beauty infinite. And then and there
Whatever he imagined took at once
A bodily shape; and nought conceived or done
Since life began appeared irrational,
Wanton or needless. Time,[4] the world and fate,
Material functions of each other, apt
As syllables of power and magic mind
In some self-reading riddle, as fracted bits
In self-adjusting instruments that play
Unheard ethereal music of the spheres,
Assumed their places equably; all things
Fell duly into line and dressed their ranks.

Thus art begins, as sudden as a star
In some unconstellated tract of space,
Where two extinct long-wandering orbs collide

[3] MS reading; 'They' in *Fleet Street, and Other Poems.*
[4] MS reading; 'Since' in *Fleet Street, and Other Poems.*

And smite into each other and become
A lamp of glory, no crepuscular
Uncertainty, no interval between
The old misfortune and the new delight.
And thus at once the plodder of the waste
Attains utility and finds himself
Aristocrat and patron of the road;
The artisan, an artist—aristocrat
And artist being ever[5] synonymes.
All vagabondage, all bohemianism,
All errantry, the unlicked, chrysalid
Condition of aristocracy and art,
Cut off for ever, the proud pedestrian free
Of the world, walks only now in picked resorts,
And can without a chart, without a guide,
Discover lands richer than El Dorado,
Sweeter than Beulah,[6] and with ease
Ascend secluded mountains more delectable
Than heights in ancient pilgrimages famed,
Or myth-clad hills, or summits of romance,
Old traversed roads he traverses again,
Untroubled; nothing new he sees
Except the stretch of pleasure-ground, like one
Who turns the leaves o'er of a tedious book,
Careless of verbiage, to reperuse
The single page inspired; in regions new
He goes directly to his own like beasts
That never miss the way; and having marked
A province with the beauties of his choice,
In them alone he walks, lord of the world.

[5] MS reading; 'over' in *Fleet Street, and Other Poems.*

[6] The land of heavenly joy where Pilgrim waits before entering heaven, in Bunyan's *The Pilgrim's Progress.*

41

From The Testament of Sir Simon Simplex Concerning Automobilism[1]

To go by train from one place to another
You have to brave the station's smoke and smother:
The train derides you there; 'twill never come
To pick you up, nor turn, to see you home,
A single wheel: the getting under way,
The true vexation of a holiday,
The stolid train permits you to deplore;
But with your automobile at the door—
Why, there you are, nor need you stir a foot,
Man and portmanteau instantly *en route*!
You buy a ticket if you go by train
At some offensive loophole, which you gain
After prolonged attendance in a queue—
Whatever class you take, a motley crew:
And to await one's turn, like patient Job,
Unites one with a vengeance to the Mob.
Then you may miss the train; but *you* must wait
Its advent and departure prompt or late.
The motor soothes, the railway racks, your nerves;
The train commands, the automobile serves.
The automobile nurses all caprice,
And gives the longest life a second lease;
Indulges indolence, and even in me
Increases individuality.
I thought and many my opinion shared
That the deceased politic[2] who declared
That all were Socialists, had told, perhaps,
A fib, exploited in a studied lapse
Of platform declamation as a sop

[1] The title of this poem has sometimes caused confusion. Though calling it a 'Testament', D. did not group it with his sequence of Testaments. It is a satiric piece, based on a prose article, 'From Totnes to Penzance', *Glasgow Herald* (25 May 1907), 11. The poem appeared in *New Age* (28 Mar. 1908), 429–30, and in *Fleet Street, and Other Poems*.

[2] *politic*: used as substantive, with stress on the second syllable.

To catch erratic voters on the hop,
The strained politeness of a caustic mind,
A dead-lift effort to say something kind.
'Twas more than that: not only had we learned
To suffer Socialism; our souls discerned
A something fine about it; egoists even
Perceived therein at last a mundane heaven.

'Life is a railway journey', genius thought—
(The erring genius very cheaply bought
With gilded apples of Asphaltites)[3]—
'Thieves bearing swag, and poets sprouting bays,
The ring, the cabinet, scortatory[4] dames,
Bishops, sectarians of a myriad names,
Bankers and brokers, merchants, mendicants,
Booked in the same train like a swarm of ants;
First, second, third, class, mass and mob expressed
Together to the Islands of the Blest—
Each passenger provided with a groat
To pass the Stygian stile for Charon's[5] boat.
Or broad or narrow as the gauge may run,
None leaves the track without disaster; none
Escapes a single stoppage on the way;
And none arrives before his neighbour may.
In the guard's van my sacred luggage knocks
Against the tourist's traps, the bagman's box;
And people with inferior aims to mine
Partake the rapid transit of the line.
But this is culture of the social school,
And teaches me to lead my life by rule
Empirical, of positive descent
And altruistic self-embezzlement.
Life *is* a railway journey: I rejoice
That folk whose purpose, visage, clothes and voice

[3] The allusion is to the proverbial 'Dead Sea Fruit', or 'Apples of Sodom'.

[4] *scortatory*: lustful.

[5] Charon is the old man who ferries the souls of the dead over the river Styx, requiring a coin as payment (classical mythology).

Offend me will continue to offend
In the same train until the journey's end.'

So spoke the genius in pathetic rage.—
The socialistic and the railway age
Were certainly coeval; machinery too
Equated communism; and every new
Development of electricity
Was welcomed by the Mob with three times three,
Convinced the world at last was through the wood—
Right through to Universal Brotherhood!

Conceive it:—Universal Brotherhood.
With everybody feeble, kind and good!
I, even I, Sir Simon Simplex, know
The world would end to-day if that were so.
What spur does man require, what stinging zest
To do still better than his level best?
Why, enemies; and if he has them not
He must unearth and beat them till they're hot;
For only enmity can train and trounce
The cortex and the muscle to an ounce.
Let Socialists deny, mistaking peace,
That only with the world will warfare cease;
When *we* behold the battle-flags unfurled
We know the fates phlebotomise the world,
And alternate with peace's patent pill,
The old heroic cure for every ill.

Life was a railway journey; foe and friend,
Infected with nostalgy of the end,
Awaited patiently the crack of doom;
But thank the powers that be, the motor boom,
Predestined to postpone the judgment-day,
Arrived in time to show a better way.
And when the automobile came we found
Our incorrupt opinion safe and sound,
Inoculated only by the schism,
For ever proof against all Socialism.
The motor stops the decadence: not all

Are in the same train with the prodigal,
The Christian scientist, the *souteneur*,[6]
The Gothamite, the man from anywhere,
Domestic Gill and idiomatic Jack,
The wheedling knave, the sneak, the hectoring quack;
The man of broader mind and farther goal
Is not entrained with Lubin Littlesoul;
Your gentleman by birth with quickened sense,
Refined requirements and abundant pence,
And men of faculty and swelling aim
Who conquer riches, power, position, fame,
Are not entrained with loafers, quibblers, cranks,
Nor with the Mob who never leave the ranks,
With plodding dullness, unambitious ease,
And discontented incapacities.

. . . Wealth and the crafty hand
That gathers wealth had always at command
Horse-carriages for private travel, but
The pace had got beyond that leisured rut;
Class, mass and mob for fifty years and more
Had all to travel in the jangling roar
Of railways, the nomadic caravan
That stifled individual mind in man,
Till automobilism arose at last!
Now with the splendid periods of the past
Our youthful century is proudly linked;
And things that Socialism supposed extinct,
Degree, nobility and noble strife,
A form, a style, a privacy in life
Will reappear; and, crowning nature's plan,
The individual and the gentleman
In England reassume his lawful place
And vindicate the greatness of the race.

[6] *souteneur*: pimp.

42
Snow[1]

I

'Who affirms that crystals are alive?'
I affirm it, let who will deny:—
Crystals are engendered, wax and thrive,
Wane and wither: I have seen them die.

Trust me, masters, crystals have their day
Eager to attain the perfect norm,
Lit with purpose, potent to display
Facet, angle, colour, beauty, form.

II

Water-crystals need for flower and root
Sixty clear degrees, no less, no more;
Snow, so fickle, still in this acute
Angle thinks, and learns no other lore:

Such its life, and such its pleasure is,
Such its art and traffic, such its gain,
Evermore in new conjunctions this
Admirable angle to maintain.

Crystalcraft in every flower and flake
Snow exhibits, of the welkin free:
Crystalline are crystals for the sake,
All and singular, of crystalry.

Yet does every crystal of the snow
Individualise, a seedling sown
Broadcast, but instinct with power to grow
Beautiful in beauty of its own.

[1] Based on a prose article, 'Urban Snow', *Glasgow Herald* (5 Jan. 1907), 7. Some of the ideas for the article and poem may have come from passages in Robert Chambers's *Book of Days* (London, 1863–4) and Ernst Haeckel's *Wonders of Life*, trans. Joseph McCabe (London, 1904).

Every flake with all its prongs and dints
  Burns ecstatic as a new-lit star:
Men are not more diverse, finger-prints
  More dissimilar than snow-flakes are.

Worlds of men and snow endure, increase,
  Woven of power and passion to defy
Time and travail: only races cease,
  Individual men and crystals die.

III

Jewelled shapes of snow whose feathery showers,
  Fallen or falling wither at a breath,
All afraid are they, and loth as flowers
  Beasts and men to tread the way to death.

Once I saw upon an object-glass,
  Martyred underneath a microscope,
One elaborate snow-flake slowly pass,
  Dying hard, beyond the reach of hope.

Still from shape to shape the crystal changed,
  Writhing in its agony; and still,
Less and less elaborate, arranged
  Potently the angle of its will.

Tortured to a simple final form,
  Angles six and six divergent beams,
Lo, in death it touched the perfect norm
  Verifying all its crystal dreams!

IV

Such the noble tragedy of one
  Martyred snow-flake. Who can tell the fate
Heinous and uncouth of showers undone,
  Fallen in cities!—showers that expiate

Errant lives from polar worlds adrift
  Where the great millennial snows abide;

Castaways from mountain-chains that lift
  Snowy summits in perennial pride;

Nomad snows, or snows in evil day
  Born to urban ruin, to be tossed,
Trampled, shovelled, ploughed, and swept away
  Down the seething sewers: all the frost

Flowers of heaven melted up with lees,
  Offal, recrement,[2] but every flake
Showing to the last in fixed degrees
  Perfect crystals for the crystal's sake.

V

Usefulness of snow is but a chance
  Here in temperate climes with winter sent,
Sheltering earth's prolonged hibernal trance:
  All utility is accident.

Sixty clear degrees the joyful snow,
  Practising economy of means,
Fashions endless beauty in, and so
  Glorifies the universe with scenes

Arctic and antarctic: stainless shrouds,
  Ermine woven in silvery frost, attire
Peaks in every land among the clouds
  Crowned with snows to catch the morning's fire.

[2] *recrement*: refuse or waste.

43

Two Dogs[1]

Two dogs on Bournemouth beach: a mongrel, one,
With spaniel plainest on the palimpsest,
The blur of muddled stock; the other, bred,
With tapering muzzle, rising brow, strong jaw—
A terrier to the tail's expressive tip,
Magnetic, nimble, endlessly alert.

The mongrel, wet and shivering, at my feet
Deposited a wedge of half-inch board,
A foot in length and splintered at the butt;
Withdrew a yard and crouched in act to spring,
While to and fro between his wedge and me
The glancing shuttle of his eager look
A purpose wove. The terrier, ears a-cock,
And neck one curve of sheer intelligence,
Stood sentinel: no sound, no movement, save
The mongrel's telegraphic eyes, bespoke
The object of the canine pantomime.

I stooped to grasp the wedge, knowing the game;
But like a thing uncoiled the mongrel snapped
It off, and promptly set it out again,
The terrier at his quarters, every nerve
Waltzing inside his lithe rigidity.

'More complex than I thought!' Again I made
To seize the wedge; again the mongrel won,
Whipped off the jack, relaid it, crouched and watched,
The terrier at attention all the time.
I won the third bout: ere the mongrel snapped
His toy, I stayed my hand; he halted, half
Across the neutral ground, and in his[2] pause

[1] Based on a prose article, 'A Railway Journey', *Glasgow Herald* (27 Apr. 1907), 9. The poem appeared in the *Westminster Gazette* (17 Oct. 1908), 2, and in *Fleet Street, and Other Poems.*

[2] *his*: MS reading; 'the' in *Fleet Street, and Other Poems.*

Of doubt I seized the prize. A vanquished yelp
From both; and then intensest vigilance.

Together, when I tossed the wedge, they plunged
Before it reached the sea. The mongrel, out
Among the waves, and standing to them, meant
Heroic business; but the terrier dodged
Behind, adroitly scouting in the surf,
And seized the wedge, rebutted by the tide,
In shallow water, while the mongrel searched
The English Channel on his hind-legs poised.
The terrier laid the trophy at my feet;
And neither dog protested when I took
The wedge: the overture of their marine
Diversion had been played out once for all.

A second match the reckless mongrel won,
Vanishing twice under the heavy surf,
Before he found and brought the prize to land.
Then for an hour the aquatic sport went on,
And still the mongrel took the heroic rôle,
The terrier hanging deftly in the rear.
Sometimes the terrier when the mongrel found
Betrayed a jealous scorn, as who should say,
'Your hero's always a vulgarian! Pah!'
But when the mongrel missed, after a fight
With such a sea of troubles, and saw the prize
Grabbed by the terrier in an inch of surf,
He seemed entirely satisfied, and watched
With more pathetic vigilance the cast
That followed.

'Once a passion, mongrel, this
Retrieving of a stick', I told the brute,
'Has now become a vice with you. Go home!
Wet to the marrow and palsied with the cold,
You won't give in, and, good or bad, you've earned
My admiration. Go home now and get warm,
And the best bone in the pantry.' As I talked
I stripped the water from his hybrid coat,

Laughed and made much of him—which mortified
The funking terrier.

'I'm despised, it seems!'
The terrier thought, 'My cleverness (my feet
Are barely wet!) beside the mongrel's zeal
Appears timidity. This biped's mad
To pet the stupid brute. Yap! Yah!' He seized
The wedge and went; and at his heels at once,
Without a thought of me, the mongrel trudged.

Along the beach, smokers of cigarettes,
All sixpenny-novel-readers to a man,
Attracted Master Terrier. Again the wedge,
Passed to the loyal mongrel, was teed with care;
Again the fateful overture began.
Upon the fourth attempt, and not before,
And by a feint at that, the challenged youth
(Most equable, be sure, of all the group:
Allow the veriest dog to measure men!)
Secured the soaked and splintered scrap of deal.
Thereafter, as with me, the game progressed,
The breathless, shivering mongrel, rushing out
Into the heavy surf, there to be tossed
And tumbled like floating bunch of kelp,
While gingerly the terrier picked his steps
Strategic in the rear, and snapped the prize
Oftener than his more adventurous, more
Romantic, more devoted rival did.
The uncomfortable moral glares at one!
And, further, in the mongrel's wistful mind
A primitive idea darkly wrought:
Having once lost the prize in the overture
With his bipedal rival, he felt himself
In honour and in conscience bound to plunge
For ever after it at the winner's will.
But the smart terrier was an Overdog,
And knew a trick worth two of that. He thought—
If canine cerebration works like ours,
And I interpret canine mind aright—

'Let men and mongrels worry and wet their coats!
I use my brains and choose the better part.
Quick-witted ease and self-approval lift
Me miles above this anxious cur, absorbed,
Body and soul, in playing a game I win
Without an effort. And yet the mongrel seems
The happier dog. How's that? Belike, the old
Compensatory principle again.
I have pre-eminence and conscious worth;
And he his[3] power to fling himself away
For anything or nothing. Men and dogs,
What an unfathomable world it is!'

[3] *his*: MS reading; 'has' in *Fleet Street, and Other Poems.*

44

The Wasp[1]

Once as I went by rail to Epping Street,
Both windows being open, a wasp flew in;
Through the compartment swung and almost out
Scarce seen, scarce heard; but dead against the pane
Entitled 'Smoking', did the train's career
Arrest her passage. Such a wonderful
Impervious transparency, before
That palpitating moment, had never yet
Her airy voyage thwarted. Undismayed,
With diligence incomparable, she sought
An exit, till the letters like a snare
Entangled her; or else the frosted glass
And signature indelible appeared
The key to all the mystery: there she groped,
And flirted petulant wings, and fiercely sang
A counter-spell against the sorcery,
The sheer enchantment that inhibited
Her access to the world—her birthright there!
So visible, and so beyond her reach!
Baffled and raging like a tragic queen,
She left at last the stencilled tablet; roamed
The pane a while to cool her regal ire,
Then tentatively touched the window-frame:
Sure footing still, though rougher than the glass;
Dissimilar in texture, and so obscure!

Perplexed now by opacity with foot and wing
She coasted up and down the wood and worked
Her wrath to passion-point again. Then from the frame
She slipped by chance into the open space
Left by the lowered sash:—the world once more
In sight! She paused; she closed her wings, and felt
The air with learned antennæ for the smooth

[1] This first appeared in the *Athenæum* (19 Dec. 1908), 789, and in *Fleet Street, and Other Poems.*

Resistance that she knew now must belong
To such mysterious transparences.
No foothold? Down she fell—six inches down!—
Hovered a second, dazed and dubious still;
Then soared away a captive queen set free.

45

From The Testament of John Davidson[1] [In Defence of Suicide]

Who kills
Himself subdues the conqueror of kings:
Exempt from death is he who takes his life:
My time has come. The native energy
Whereby I exorcised fantastical
Immutability, and in my own
Resemblance reproduced the plastic world,
Beginning to relent, abates the thrust
And tension of my thought, discharges love,
Unwinds the poignant charm of living, frees
Imagination—known eternity,
Confined in lightning, light, or radiant soul,
That breaks atomic chrysalids unseen,
Unthinkable, but certain and innate—
To melt into the ether, and to be
Transmuted to infinity again.
We are the plunging fire, the molten seed
That gladdened, swelled and rent the generous wombs
We harboured in—most wilful, fateful births,
Predestined by ourselves before the world
Or time began, and wholly answerable;
For had we not, beyond all yea or nay,
Escaped alive among the myriad germs
Devoutly squandered from abundant reins
To dower a woman's body with delight,
We had not been. By my own will alone
The ethereal substance, which I am, attained,

[1] This was begun in the early months of 1908 with the encouragement of Grant Richards, who planned to issue D.'s five Testaments in one volume. But Richards had lost the copyright of the first four Testaments as a result of his bankruptcy in 1904, and the idea had to be abandoned. The poem was published on its own, with a lengthy prose dedication 'To the Peers Temporal of the United Kingdom of Great Britain and Ireland' in autumn 1908.

And now by my own sovereign will, forgoes,
Self-consciousness; and thus are men supreme:
No other living thing can choose to die.
This franchise and this high prerogative
I show the world:—Men are the Universe
Aware at last, and must not live in fear,
Slaves of the seasons, padded, bolstered up,
Clystered[2] and drenched and dieted and drugged;
Or hateful victims of senility,
Toothless and like an infant checked and schooled;
Or in the dungeon of a sick room drained
By some tabescent[3] horror in their prime;
But when the tide of life begins to turn,
Before the treason of the ebbing wave
Divulges refuse and the barren shore,
Upon the very period of the flood,
Stand out to sea and bend our weathered sails
Against the sunset, valiantly resolved
To win the haven of eternal night.

[2] *clystered*: given an enema.

[3] *tabescent*: causing emaciation.

Epilogue—The Last Journey

I felt the world a-spinning on its nave,
  I felt it sheering blindly round the sun;
I felt the time had come to find a grave:
  I knew it in my heart my days were done.
I took my staff in hand; I took the road,
And wandered out to seek my last abode.
    Hearts of gold and hearts of lead
      Sing it yet in sun and rain,
    'Heel and toe from dawn to dusk,
      Round the world and home again.'

O long before the bere was steeped for malt,
  And long before the grape was crushed for wine,
The glory of the march without a halt,
  The triumph of a stride like yours and mine
Was known to folk like us, who walked about,
To be the sprightliest cordial out and out!
    Folk like us, with hearts that beat,
      Sang it too in sun and rain—
    'Heel and toe from dawn to dusk,
      Round the world and home again.'

My feet are heavy now, but on I go,
  My head erect beneath the tragic years.
The way is steep, but I would have it so;
  And dusty, but I lay the dust with tears,
Though none can see me weep: alone I climb
The rugged path that leads me out of time—
    Out of time and out of all,
      Singing yet in sun and rain,
    'Heel and toe from dawn to dusk,
      Round the world and home again.'

Farewell the hope that mocked, farewell despair
  That went before me still and made the pace.
The earth is full of graves, and mine was there
  Before my life began, my resting-place;

And I shall find it out and with the dead
Lie down for ever, all my sayings said—
    Deeds all done and songs all sung,
        While others chant in sun and rain,
    'Heel to toe from dawn to dusk,
        Round the world and home again.'

46

[Cain's Final Blessing], *from* Cain[1]

God's curse is on us; and we make it do.
Our errant life is not unhappy; fear,
That harrows others, is to us unknown,
Being close to God by reason of His curse.
Sometimes I think that God Himself is cursed,
For all His things go wrong. We cannot guess;
He is very God of God, not God of men:
We feel His power, His inhumanity;
Yet, being men, we fain would think Him good.
Since in imagination we conceive
A merciful, a gracious God of men,
It may be that our prayer and innocent life
Will shame Him into goodness in the end.
Meantime His vengeance is upon us; so,
My blessing and God's curse be with you all.

[1] One of D.'s last poems. He intended it to be one of a series of five monologues—'Cain', 'Judas', 'Cæsar Borgia', 'Calvin', and 'Cromwell'—but only 'Cain' was written. He included it with the manuscript of *Fleet Street, and Other Poems*.

PROSE

EXTRACTS FROM ARTICLES ON POETRY

Pre-Shakespearianism

THE newspaper is one of the most potent factors in moulding the character of contemporary poetry. Perhaps it was first of all the newspaper that couched the eyes of poetry. Burns's eyes were open. Blake's also for a time; and Wordsworth had profound insight into the true character of man and of the world; but all the rest saw men as trees walking; Tennyson and Browning are Shakespearian. The prismatic cloud that Shakespeare hung out between poets and the world! It was the newspapers, I think, that brought us round to what may be called an order of Pre-Shakespearianism. It was out of the newspapers that Thomas Hood got 'The Song of the Shirt'—in its place the most important English poem of the nineteenth century; the 'woman in unwomanly rags plying her needle and thread' is the type of the world's misery. 'The Song of the Shirt' is the most terrible poem in the English language. Only a high heart and strong brain broken on the wheel of life, but master of its own pain and anguish, able to jest in the jaws of death, could have sung this song, of which every single stanza wrings the heart. Poetry passed by on the other side. It could not endure the woman in unwomanly rags. It hid its head like the fabled ostrich in some sand-bed of Arthurian legend, or took shelter in the paradoxical optimism of 'The Ring and the Book'. It is true William Morris stood by her when the priest and the Levite passed by. He stood by her side, he helped her; but he hardly saw her, nor could he show her as she is. 'Mother and Son', his greatest poem, and a very great poem, is a vision of a deserted Titaness in London streets; there was a veil also between him and the world, although in another sense, with his elemental Sigurds, he is the truest of all Pre-Shakespearians. But the woman in unwomanly rags, and all the insanity and iniquity of which she is the type, will now be sung. Poetry will concern itself with her and hers for some time to come. The offal of the world is being said in statistics, in prose fiction: it is besides going to be sung. James Thomson sang it; and others are doing so. Will it be of any avail? We cannot tell. Nothing that has been done avails. Poor-laws, charity organisations, dexterously hold the wound open, or tenderly and hopelessly skin over the cancer. But there it is in the streets, the hospitals, the poor-houses, the prisons; it is the flood that surges about our feet, it rises breast-high. And it will be sung in all keys and voices. Poetry has other functions, other aims; but this also has become its province. (*Speaker*, 19 (28 Jan. 1899), 107–8.)

Reply to the Critics

I.

'A. T. Q. C.'[1] selects for animadversion certain texts from my article called at a venture 'Pre-Shakespearianism', ignoring the context—the well-known method of the heresy hunter.

I insist in my article that poets—some poets, at least—are now aware of the multitudinous misery in which the ease of the few is rooted, and that it will be sung; but I am careful to add, 'Poetry has other functions, other aims'.

'Popularity' and 'obscenity' are not mentioned by me, nor were they in all my thoughts. I must refer the reader to the last poem in 'The Last Ballad, and other Poems',[2] for what I mean by 'the offal of the world'.

I think it is most inartistic, most unpoetical, most unwise, to look at the world through The Tempest. It would be as artistic, as poetical, as wise to look at our enormous London through the London of Chaucer's time and say, 'London is small and white and clean.' (*Speaker*, 19 (18 Feb. 1899), 206.)

II.

'A. T. Q. C.'[3] sums up his argument under three heads as follows:—

'1. The first business of poetry, and that for which she is pre-eminently fitted by all her methods, is to express beauty.

2. That this business logically includes research after spiritual truth, which is the most beautiful thing in the world.

3. But that it has by no reasonable showing anything to do, save accidentally, with 'phenomenal truth', which science can handle much better, and which in constructive art becomes mere imitation of appearance. For this accuracy may as easily result in ugliness as in beauty, if not more easily.'

[1] Arthur T. Quiller-Couch had challenged D.'s views on poetry in 'A Literary Causerie', *Speaker*, 19 (11 Feb. 1899), 178.

[2] 'Eclogue: Votary and Artist' in the present volume.

[3] This was a reply to Quiller-Couch's arguments in 'A Literary Causerie', *Speaker*, 19 (25 Feb. 1899), 232.

I reply:—

1. The function of poetry, as I understand it, is to pierce to what may be behind phenomena.

2. I am not yet certain that spiritual truth is the most beautiful thing in the world.

3. Behind phenomena I have found an inexorable irony. Phenomena themselves are often beautiful; but perhaps they are only accidentally connected with spiritual truth, skin-deep, the complexion of this irony. I may ultimately find that irony includes beauty, and is greater than beauty. If poetry, aided by science, should find that truth is ugly, poetry will say so; but, as nothing is ugly to science, perhaps poetry may learn a lesson. (*Speaker*, 19 (4 Mar. 1899), 260.)

III.

Worshipful Irony, the profound 'Irony of fate', is doubtless responsible for Renanism,[1] and all 'isms, but is derived from none of these.

It is centric, the adamantine axis of the universe. At its poles are the illusions we call matter and spirit, day and night, pleasure and pain, beauty and ugliness. By it our enterprises are whirled away from our most resolved intentions. A playwright, wearing out his life in an abortive effort to found a country family, makes the literature of the world Shakespearian centuries after his death; the Pilgrim Fathers colonise America in the name of the Highest—that Tammany may flourish in New York; and out of the beautiful Shakespearianism may come evil; out of Tammany, good.

Irony is the enigma within the enigma, the open secret, the only answer vouchsafed the eternal riddle. (*Speaker*, 19 (22 Apr. 1899), 455.)

[1] A philosophy that challenges the theory of the greatest good for the greatest number with an aristocratic belief in the superiority of the few—from the French philosopher Ernest Renan (1823–92).

The Art of Poetry

Poetry is the most empirical of all the arts; in a sense every poet is a charlatan; he can give no authority except his own experience, his own imagination; in the last resort he can give no authority at all; he cannot tell: it was the Muse. Whether he be artificer or artist, and the true poet is always both, it is liberty of utterance he seeks. Poetry is the least artificial of all the arts; it is at its best when it is most archaic. This is not a matter of obsolete words; rather it is the eschewing of libraries, a getting back to the earth divested, saving the harp and sword, of all the inventions of man's hands and mind. Thus the freest utterance is always to be found in the narrative or the drama. Subconsciousness, which the poet singing in his own character inevitably obscures—that is to say, the eternal, the voice of the species—becomes audible in personation. The Elizabethan–Jacobean age, the great period of the drama, is also the great period of poetry, when every aid to free and full utterance was employed in the disdain of art. It was in *The Spanish Tragedy* that Kyd revealed the new and excellent way of the madman. Here was liberty at last; everything could be said; and the kernel of the world appear through the rent in the heart, the crack in the mind. Hieronimo announces the woe of the awakened intelligence trembling on the verge of madness in three lines, three crude lines that are not surpassed by any piercing utterance of Hamlet, Timon, or Lear:—

> This toils my body, this consumeth age,
> That only I to all men just must be,
> And neither gods nor men be just to me.

It is a cry wrung from the inmost heart. These words do not occur in the additional matter; they are Kyd's, and they are the cognisance of Elizabethan tragedy. (*Speaker*, 19 (4 Feb. 1899), 153–4.)

Rhyme

At its best, rhyme is a decadent mode, although great ages and great poets have made it the vehicle for crescive work. It is a special flattery of the external ear; it is as rouge on the cheek and belladonna on the eye; or it is an excrescence like a sixth finger, 'a wasteful and ridiculous excess': it is commonly either deceptive or meaningless. I am not thinking of bad poetry; but of the best.

Let me illustrate. Here is the first quatrain of Shakespeare's seventy-third sonnet:—

> 'That time of year thou mays't in me behold
> When yellow leaves, or none, or few, do hang
> Upon those boughs which shake against the cold,
> Bare ruin'd choirs, where late the sweet birds sang.'

The rhymes of this quatrain toll like a death-bell: we pass from a sombre forest to a dim cathedral; the fancy is overwhelmed with vision, both detailed, and indefinite, in order to bring the rhymes about; there is a feeling of effort, as of a thing achieved; and it is the rhyme that achieves; it is not the poet, not the poetry, but the rhyme that requires this laborious 'or none, or few'; it is the rhyme that requires those superbly imagined 'boughs which shake against the cold' to shift at once as by the waft of a rococo conjurer's wand into 'bare ruin'd choirs'. Yet it is beautiful, it is poignant; it entertains the fancy, fills the eye and ear, and touches the soul.

But, now, let Macbeth say the same thing without rhyme:—

> 'My way of life
> Is fallen into the sere, the yellow leaf.'

No comment; the hair of the flesh stands up and one knows henceforth and for ever there is a great gulf fixed between rhyme and blank verse.

Nevertheless the exquisite adornment of rhyme will continue to corrupt the ear of the world, the seeing ear as well as the hearing ear: it is mainly with the ear that the reader of poetry sees. A speculative writer suggested once that the eye is a degenerate organ, the malversation of some higher perceptive power, inconceivable in range and penetration. By such an analogy the ear was originally intended for vision as well as audition; the tympanum and tympanic membrane, when one considers them, are clearly a combination of mirror and sounding-board. Why the mirror remains inoperative we cannot say, since no blind beggar has, up to this time of writing, developed vision by light refracted through the auditory canal; but the reader of poetry knows very well that the optic nerve responds like a taut string to the rhymes that vibrate in the membranous labyrinth of the ear; and he knows also that the prompt vision flashed on the inward eye by the percussion of rhyme has injured the palate of this double sense of seeing and hearing, so that the subtler sound and loftier sight transmitted by the rhythm of blank verse are hardly possible now to his over-stimulated, frayed, and angry senses. Poetry is therefore as little understood as it ever was, rhyme—as necessary to the general verse-reader as brandy to the brandy-drinker—being, again as I say it, only an ornament. A sense of shame, indeed, struggles vainly towards a blush in the cheeks of the many-headed monster, when it turns its galaxy of eyes on a page of blank verse; its subconscious feeling is of something indecorous, if not indecent. The feeling is just: blank verse is nude poetry, barbarous and beautiful, or athletic and refined, but always naked and unashamed. Civilisation, which in all countries is in great part a development and sanction of every kind of stupidity and misconception, could perhaps be helped out of its utter artistic perdition in England by a great thing native here, blank verse, namely; and by another great thing, which we should have to import, sculpture. But that could only be brought about as an accompaniment and result of some great national movement when the minds and imaginations of all men are fused into one mood of aspiration, and so uplifted into unwonted power. (*Outlook*, 15 (8 Apr. 1905); revised as 'On Poetry', in *Holiday, and Other Poems*).

Wordsworth's Immorality and Mine

Poetry is immoral. It will state any and every morality. It has done so. There is no passion of man or passion of Matter outside its province. It will expound with equal zest the twice incestuous intrigue of Satan, Sin, and Death, and the discarnate adoration of Dante for the most beautified lady in the world's record. There is no horror of deluge, fire, plague, or war it does not rejoice to utter; no evanescent hue, or scent, or sound, it cannot catch, secure, and reproduce in word and rhythm. The worship of Aphrodite and the worship of the Virgin are impossible without its ministration. It will celebrate the triumph of the pride of life riding to victory roughshod over friend and foe, and the flame-clad glory of the martyr who lives in obloquy and dies in agony for an idea or a dream. Poetry is a statement of the world and of the Universe as the world can know it. Sometimes it is of its own time: sometimes it is ahead of time, reaching forward to a new and newer understanding and interpretation. In the latter case poetry is not only immoral in the Universal order; but also in relation to its own division of time: a great poet is very apt to be, for his own age and time, a great immoralist. This is a hard saying in England, where the current meaning of immorality is so narrow, nauseous, and stupid. I wish to transmute this depreciated word, to make it so eminent that men shall desire to be called immoralists. To be immoral is to be different . . .

Wordsworth had to think and imagine the world and the universe for himself: for him the creeds were outworn; for him 'the smug routine and things allowed', in which the common mind and imagination and the estates of the realm live in most ages, were a dungeon and miasma. The imagination of Wordsworth could not breathe in any Greek mythology, any Christian Heaven and Hell, or theological system of the Universe. Out of all the mythologies, pagan and Christian, he culled this one thing only—the idea of spirit: which he whittled down finally in the ninth book of 'The Excursion' to an 'active principle'—no longer a poetical but a metaphysical idea. Now, metaphysic is an aborted poetry. Poetry is concrete, requiring the exercise of all the material powers of body, mind, and soul, which, co-operating, are imagination. I have to use these words 'mind' and 'soul', because for what I wish to say there is as yet no language. I hold that men can think and imagine things for which there are no words: and that men must attend upon the expression of these things before all others: that these unsaid things are of more moment than all the literature and religion of the past: and that these things can in the first instance be said only by the poet, by one who makes words mean what he, that is, what Matter chooses. The mind, separating itself from the body and the soul, can transmute a figure of speech into a category; indeed, there is probably no figure of speech that could not be petrified into a metaphysic: metaphysics are the fossil remains of dead poetries. Also, the soul can separate itself from the body and the mind, and petrify a figure of speech into a theology: creeds are the fossil remains of dead religions. The body, the static and dynamic integer of which mind and soul are only exponents, is held in profound dis-esteem by both metaphysic and theology. The metaphysician says, 'The Universe is thought'; the theologian says, 'The Universe is soul.' It is as if one were to say 'amber is electricity', or 'iron is sound', or 'the spindrift is the sea', or 'this sure and firm-set earth is a word': all possible figures of speech, and therefore all liable in the hands of a pedant to be erected into a dogma. That was the tragedy of Wordsworth; his poetry became a pedantry. It was not age—a man may be a poet at eighty; it was not disease, as Wordsworth's health lasted to the end—besides, having once known what health and strength are, a man may be a poet although glued to the floor with consumption of the spinal marrow; it was not poverty, for Wordsworth was frugal, nor ever knew the hell it is to have to write for bread—besides, a man may be a poet starving in a London suburb: it was the want of a great audience and the world's applause that left Wordsworth to the pernicious obsession of a metaphysic, dried up his poetry and made him at last little better than a moralist. But whenever imagination had its way, when his powers of body, mind and soul were in equipollence and co-operating, Wordsworth's immorality could be as free as Shakespeare's or Burns's, and could disport itself with a *naïveté*, as in 'The Farmer of Tilsbury Vale', impossible to Shakespeare and Burns, who were, both of them, men of the world; and no speech of Falstaff or of Hamlet, no song of the Jolly Beggars, approaches the stark utterance in 'Rob Roy's Grave' of that immutable immorality which is the inmost complexion of the world. (*Outlook*, 15 (10 June 1905), 834–5; and (17 June 1905), 873–4; revised as Preface to *The Theatrocrat*).

LETTERS

LOCATION OF LETTERS

1. Glasgow University Library.
2. Bodleian Library, Oxford.
3. Princeton University Library.
4. Glasgow University Library.
5. Glasgow University Library.
6. Glasgow University Library.
7. University of Texas, at Austin.
8. Bodleian Library, Oxford.
9. University of Texas, at Austin.
10. The British Library.
11. Glasgow University Library.
12. Glasgow University Library.
13. Glasgow University Library.
14. Glasgow University Library.
15. The British Library.
16. The British Library.
17. Merton College, Oxford.
18. Merton College, Oxford.
19. Princeton University Library.
20. Merton College, Oxford.

1

To William Symington McCormick[1]

[June 1890] (extract)

2 Alfred Terrace,
Park Ridings,
London N.
Monday

My dear McCormick,

. . . You needn't envy me; I'm only a devil, writing work for other men; it's better than teaching, it's *better* than reviewing and I'm satisfied in the meantime. I might be earning more money and getting some kind of reputation if I were working independently, but the other way is certain and so I hold on to it for a while. *Perfervid* may do some good; but I don't really know, it went a-begging so long that I've lost conceit of it. I don't know what like Harry Furniss's[2] illustrations are, but they were done *con amore*, the publisher tells me, as he thought the book very amusing: his name will certainly give the book a chance, and a certain sale. Publishers are spending £200 on it, £30 to come to me.

I do not know whether I should say that I am happy developing a faculty for reading-writing. Since January besides leaders for the *Herald* and papers for the *Speaker*, I have written to order two volumes, and have just made up my mind to write half of a three volume novel in six weeks—a mere bagatelle to the professional novel writer. In the second volume and in the prospective novel my name will appear as joint-author. Have you read 'The Fatal Phryne', 'The Pit-town Coronet' or 'Susan Ross's Marriage'? F. C. Phillips[3] and C. J. Wills[4] are the names on the title pages of the first and third. Wills, the man who is now devilling me, tells me that he wrote the whole of 'The Fatal Phryne; and most of 'Susan Ross'. 'The Pit town Coronet' is his own. Well, he naturally wants to sever his connection with Phillips, the *fainéant*, and to take me on as his collaborator. Hence the pyramids. You will gather that I have little time to go about. I have seen Robert Buchanan,[5] William Sharp,[6] Mathilde Blind,[7] a certain John M. Robertson,[8] a certain Rousel[9] or something, French painter and that's all. Sharp has a crowd coming about him on Sundays. He is a good-natured man, but his wife has learnt her lesson, and 'got 'em on'—I mean the breeches as well as the bluestockings and the spectacles. Of course, old Van Laun,[7] whom I will take you to the moment you come to London if you don't mind, I see often. I'm in difficulty about him just now; he wants me to collaborate with him on a shilling dreadful, and after that on a three volume novel, but I like neither of his subjects, and I don't believe I could make anything of them.

My home consists of six match-boxes fastened insecurely together. There is a strip of hard clay called a garden in which I have been trying to sow some annuals, but I find the soil so well stocked with bottles and crockery that there is little room for candytuft. We lead a semi-patriarchal life here—Adam delves and Eve spins, and Cain and Abel are well, and the first woman sends her love.

Yours ever,
John Davidson.

[1] (1859–1930), Chaucer scholar and Professor of English Literature at University College, Dundee; he and D. met in Prof. Nichol's circle at Glasgow University in the late 1870s or early 1880s.

[2] (1854–1925), caricature artist.

[3] Francis Charles Philips (1849–1921), novelist and dramatist.

[4] Charles James Wills (1842–1912), journalist and author.

[5] (1841–1901), poet and novelist, who corresponded with John Nichol.

[6] (1855–1905), author and Celtic romanticist, who corresponded with John Nichol.

[7] (1841–96), poet whose *The Ascent of Man* (1889) combined poetry and science. She was a friend of the Sharps.

[8] (1856–1933), editor *National Reformer.*

[9] Théodore Rousel (1847–1926), painter influenced by James Whistler (1834–1903).

[10] Henri van Laun (1820–96), polyglot Dutchman who translated Molière. D. may have been introduced to him by the poet and socialist John Barlas (1860–1914), with whom he made friends when they were both teaching at Morrison's Academy, Crieff, in Scotland.

2

To Bertram Dobell[1]

25 November 1890

2 Alfred Terrace,
Park Ridings,
Hornsey,
London N.

My dear Mr Dobell,

I told you that I had read Thomson's 'Life',[2] and then I asked you 'if you had known Thomson'. And yet it is true that I have read his life, and the 'Memoir' to 'A Voice from the Nile',[3] the story of his difficulties in finding a publisher and his success at last being perfectly clear in my mind. One name had escaped my memory, and I asked the owner of that name 'if he had known Thomson'.

The gift of Thomson's books from you makes me feel as if in some measure they had come from himself; and your appreciation of my own attempts which I valued much before is now quite priceless to me.

I am
Sincerely yours
John Davidson.

[1] (1842–1914), second-hand bookseller, who procured publication of James Thomson's *The City of Dreadful Night, and Other Poems* (London, 1880).

[2] Henry Salt, *The Life of James Thomson* (London, 1889).

[3] James Thomson, *A Voice from the Nile, and Other Poems.* With a 'Memoir' by Bertram Dobell (London, 1884).

3

To Miss Menzies McArthur[1]

[1890]

2 Alfred Terrace,
Park Ridings,
London N.
Monday

My dear Meem,

I haven't the least right to advise you, or anybody, especially about marriage, at least from the economical point of view, having failed and failed again, although now I think we shall get on slowly, but without another collapse. But I would like to talk to you, if you will let me.

Isn't it the case that the marriage ceremony is a minor detail when a man and woman elect to spend their lives together, and that the promise made to each other between the kisses is the true promise of which the form of marriage is a mere ratification? Haven't you said to yourself 'I took him for better or worse when I gave him my *heart*?' Have you then the right to give him up now? If you're really certain that you gave him your heart, that is to say. Knock at the door of your heart till you find out that definitely; and I think the test should be this: if you do not now already understand, and even sympathise with him in the mistake he has made it would be well to consider the advisability of accepting the release which he could not possibly withhold. But if you feel how the man was driven and whirled by his own misery and tempted with a temporary oblivion by pleasant companions—and you do feel that, because you know the stifling horror you experienced yourself when the news came that the hope that had maintained you for two years had ended so—you will banish from your mind all blame, all anger, and even thrust pity out too, and cling to your love for him, and be absolutely careless of everything else. It is not him and his love for you that will satisfy you—you remember I don't believe in happiness but in satisfaction—but your own love for him: over that no circumstances of disaster or poverty can have any power. Your love for him, if you have it truly, is a thing that even your own will has no control over. It is a gift from heaven, that will increase with the demands made upon it.

You have had bitter trials in your life—I, for one have thought that you bore them well—and you imagined now that they were to end, and your life was to be smooth with pleasant excitements—that you were to enter into your heritage as a woman—and the cup's dashed from your lips, and I could cry for you myself. Why should this happen to you? So many others have easy pleasant lives, and never have had any need to hang their heads—what have you done that you should be tortured in this way? What does it mean at all? No; but say rather—'Here is a labour of love given to my hands, which I am thought worthy to undertake—in misery, in darkness, not seeing one step before another. My bed is not to be one of roses—to me also it is given to be a heroine—to do and to suffer something—nobody understanding, many mocking; all by myself I must go out into the night and be strong for two.' Why, Meem, my dearest, there's nothing lost yet. You've got a good head, and a strong body and a stout heart, and you're much younger than you think you are. Always think of the man in his misery in the foreign town suffering for two—because that was the terrible thing for him, that he had led you to hope and now it could not be, and chance thrust oblivion on him and he took it—and 'best men are moulded out of faults'.

If you go to Hamburgh you must marry him—but no further than the ceremony, that would be unwise; and have the right to save his money for him, and above all to meet him the moment he arrives from his next voyage. A course like this will seem absurd to those who don't know the circumstances, and you will have to gulp down some sob, it is so unlike the wedding every woman has a right to expect. But what else is there to be done. It is the only way to save the man, and yourself too, Meem. Can you for a moment look without swooning into the future without Jack Stewart?

I'm so hard up that I can't send you any money, or ask you yet to stay with us, but in a month or so, you could come and stay with us as long as you liked.

When you see Jack don't let him talk to you in the style of his letters. Shut him up with kisses. He has thought and written too much about his 'fall' as he calls it already—in his loneliness, poor chap. Tell him it's all past and forgotten, and insist on it to yourself too, until it *is* all past and forgotten. You have the future—and it hides in it joy and sorrow, but our hearts are stout for hoping, and our bodies strong for living.

Yours ever,
John Davidson.

[1] D.'s sister-in-law, whose fiancé, Jack Stewart, a sailor, had squandered all his money at sea.

4

To William Symington McCormick
[November 1891] (extract)

2 Alfred Terrace,
Park Ridings,
Hornsey
London N.
Monday

Mac of Macs,

. . . 'In a Music-Hall'—have stuck to the title—is through the press and I expect it out in a week or two. Will send a copy . . .

Have not seen, nor put myself in the way of seeing Oscar[1] since you were here. Strange reports about his robbery. Did you see that his house was broken into? Money stolen. A malicious youth pointed out the other night that there was no money to steal. Must turn in to the Café Royal some night, and hear all about it from himself.

Van Laun, whom I have seen once or twice, always refers to you with approval.

Canton[2] I have seen twice. There is no getting rid of, or resisting him. With all his turkey-cockishness he is good-natured, and insists on being on intimate terms.

Was at a Rhymers meeting on Friday in Lionel Johnson's[3] rooms. Low-ceiled rooms on third floor in Fitzroy Street, but plenty of space, walled with books and overpowering pictures by Simeon Solomon[4]. Lionel moving about among them like a minnow, or an anatomical preparation—the Absin[the] you remember. George-a-Greene,[5] the Pindar of Wakefield who translates Carducci was there; also Ernest Radford,[6] forked radish that would fain be an eagle, and who begins his books 'As my friend Walter Pater said to me on Saturday—no it was Sunday afternoon';[7] W. B. Yeats the wild Irishman, who lives on water-cress and pemmican and gets drunk on the smell of whisky, and can distinguish and separate out as subtly as death each individual cell in any literary organism; Rolleston,[8] once an Irish Adonis—now a consumptive father of four children; Dowson and Clough,[9] two rosebud poets. You must see the Rhymers when you come to London next month.

Last night went with Maggie[10]—having put off several invitations, and ashamed to do so any more in spite of the influenza—to call on Mrs. Johnston, a niece of Madame Blavatsky's:[11] a Caucasian Russian with copper hair, yellow eyelashes, and green eyes: shoulders as broad as a man's—chest like a sailor's; hips like a haystack: hands like an ape's, with an immense span between forefinger and thumb, but eloquent and smooth, soft voice, copious and grammatical English, but without 'ths' and a very odd accent. Her husband[12] who is the son of Johnston of Bally Kilbeg, the Ulster Orangeman of whom you may have heard, was in the covenanted service in India but resigned or—I'm not sure about this: he wants a pension although he's little more than a boy. He teaches sanskrit and writes for Indian papers. Mrs Johnston writes for Moscow papers, and novels in Russian magazines. At present she's translating a book of her aunt's travels into English.

When you come to London in December you would be better to take one of the rooms we looked at in Keppel Street, where

[1] Oscar Wilde (1854–1900). D. was introduced to Wilde by John Barlas in the summer of 1889.

[2] William Canton (1845–1926), General Manager of London publishing house of Isbister, formerly sub-editor at the *Glasgow Herald*; author of *The Lost Epic, and Other Poems* (1887), and *The Invisible Playmate* (1894).

[3] (1867–1902), poet and fellow Rhymer.

[4] (1840–1905), painter and member of Rossetti's circle.

[5] George Arthur Greene (1853–1921), who helped to organize the Rhymers' Club. The translations referred to were of the Italian poet Giosuè Carducci (1835–1907).

[6] (1882–1920), poet and fellow Rhymer.

[7] (1865–1939), poet. He and D. met at the Rhymers' Club.

[8] Thomas William Rolleston (1857–1920), author, journalist, and fellow Rhymer.

[9] Ernest Dowson (1867–1900), poet and fellow Rhymer. I have not been able to identify Clough.

[10] D.'s wife, Margaret McArthur (1859–1944), daughter of John McArthur, a bobbin-manufacturer and Dean of Guild of Perth, in Scotland.

[11] (1831–91), founder of the Theosophical Society.

[12] Charles Johnston (1867–1931), whose father, William Johnston, was the leader of the Ulster Orangemen. Charles was a school friend of Yeats and member of the Theosophical Society. He and D. met at the Rhymers' Club.

Parnell lodged, instead of going to a hotel. Let me know and I'll take one for you.

All well. Maggie sends her regards.
Yours ever
John Davidson.

5
To William Symington McCormick
10 January 1892

2 Alfred Terrace
Hornsey
London N.

My dear Mac,

I sent up a shout in my last letter when I was unwittingly entering a mood. A needy Irish MP has been appointed to a responsible post on the *Speaker*. In order to provide a salary for him the rate of payment is being reduced all round, and among his other duties he has taken over the magazines, the quarterlies and the library notes, cutting off two thirds of my income. The Irish minister is also on the staff of the *Sunday Sun*, T. P. O'Connor's[1] paper, and the *Speaker*, henceforth to exist mainly as a means of advertising 'Tay Pay'. Wemyss Reid[2] powerless, although retaining the title of editor—as powerless in the hands of the Irish party as the G.O.M. [Grand Old Man] himself.[3] The whole of the Rhymers' Club will now rush in—being mostly Irish—and review each other's poetry, and dance in triumph: for two years I have been reviewing them, to their disgust, with some impartiality. Nobody wrote to me, nor said a word to me; I think they are ashamed. I knew nothing of it till with the first January number a review of the magazines appeared, not by me, and none of my notes were used.

I am unable to resolve anything in the meantime. My plan for going on with my own work on the old financial basis had been formed. I have a sort of fierceness deep down in my heart; but I shall keep the devil at the stave's end.

Yours ever
John Davidson.

[1] (1848–1929), newspaper editor. D. had met him towards the end of 1891.

[2] Sir Thomas Wemyss Reid (1842–1905), editor of the *Speaker*, who gave D. his start in journalism.

[3] William Ewart Gladstone (1809–98).

6

To William Symington McCormick
30 December 1892 (extract)

2 Alfred Terrace
Park Ridings,
Hornsey N

My dear Mac,

... I think I told you that I had been driven to write poetry this year for my soul's salvation. Mathews and Lane[1]—'Welkin', you remember—are to publish it in the spring anonymously,[2] as my last poetry book was a great failure, partly owing to its intrinsic faults and partly owing to mistakes I made in distributing it. They print fifty large and three hundred small, and sell it at a net price: they promise me some money, and profess to be confident in the success of the book. It is always a considerable success to get a poetry book published without having to put your hand in your pocket. I put together a month ago a little sort of *obiter dicta* that will also be published in the spring—by Lawrence & Bullen who will I expect give something to account.[3] I have begun to enjoy my slow progress, and am quite reconciled to waiting a-long long time before I can expect much money from my books.

Thus it comes about that I won't be able to get North yet, but a time will come.

I go on with the *Speaker*, of course, reviewing all kinds of books, though still chiefly verse, and writing notes.

I saw Cramb[4] a week ago: he is well. Pringle Nichol[5] I see sometimes; but nobody else for a long while. I have a great

[1] Elkin Mathews (1851–1921) and John Lane (1854–1925), who had set up a bookshop and publishing house under the sign of the Bodley Head in Vigo Street, London, in 1887. 'Welkin' was D.'s playful rhyme on Mathews's name.

[2] *Fleet Street Eclogues*, first series (1893), which was in fact printed with D.'s name on the title-page.

[3] *Sentences and Paragraphs* (1893).

[4] John Adam Cramb (1861–1913), who tried journalism before becoming Professor of Modern History at Queen's College, London. He and D. met in John Nichol's circle at Glasgow University in the late 1870s or early 1880s. Cramb was best man at D.'s wedding on 23 Oct. 1885.

[5] John Pringle Nichol (1863–1917), John Nichol's eldest son, who was an under-

exposition of solitude come upon me—a nostalgia for the country—for change anyway, not having been out of London for fully three years. But a night in the Café Royal and thereabouts is always able to destroy this mood.

I thought when I saw your letter that it was to announce your advent—your fourth advent. Better luck next time. We shall eat steak in the Cheshire Cheese[6] at Easter I hope . . .

Yours ever
John Davidson.

graduate at Balliol College, Oxford (1863–6), and wrote *Victor Hugo: A Sketch of his Life and Work* (London, 1893).

[6] Ancient eating-house in Fleet Street where the Rhymers' Club met on Friday evenings.

7

To Richard Le Gallienne[1]

11 May 1893

20 Park Ridings[2]
Hornsey N.

My dear Le Gallienne,

I have just learned that you were the gracious critic in the *Daily Chronicle* as well as in the *Star*. I thank you again and again. Your reviews[3] have given me more pleasure than anything that has been written about book of mine [*sic*]; but I discriminate, as I am certain you would wish me to, and recognise the magnanimous speaking-trumpet of a generous man wishing to make people hear.

Have you ever considered how important speaking-trumpets are? The still small voice has no audience nowadays; God 'if a God there be', would require to use a fog-horn. I remember first thinking of this idea of a speaking-trumpet after reading Swinburne's reviews of Rossetti and Mathew Arnold; but I never was an Elizabethan.

With the deepest acknowledgment of your kind and daring words in my behalf, and much admiration of your own poetry.

I am
Yours sincerely
John Davidson.

[1] (1866–1947), who was at this time serving as reader for Mathews and Lane.

[2] Park Ridings was renumbered in 1893.

[3] Of *Fleet Street Eclogues*, first series. The reviews were: 'Books and Bookmen', *Star*, 4 May 1893, 2; and 'Pan in Fleet Street', *Daily Chronicle*, 6 May 1893, 3.

8

To Robert Bridges[1]

17 April 1894

20 Park Ridings,
Hornsey,
London, N.

Dear Mr Bridges,

The surprise and pleasure of your letter came upon me last night by the hands of John Lane at the dinner of the *Yellow Book* in an old street in Soho, in a low-ceiled room with Italian crockery and candles, and half a dozen of these new women who wear their sex on their sleeves, and a score and more of these new men who are sexless—very pleasant abominations of the time. I knew who had written the letter as soon as I saw 'Yattendon', for my acquaintance with you is of five years standing now—I have read with the keenest pleasure most of your books. Your letter was like a warning to me. For five years I have kept out of London although living and working in it, and last night at my very first step into it a high voice reminds me of 'my own endeavour'. I shall have to go on with London, because it becomes apparent to me although I have tried to get on without it, that it is impossible even to get enough reviewing to buy tobacco, unless one makes and keeps acquaintance will all kinds of bosses, strappers, and understrappers, but I shall try to be in it and not of it.

It was indeed a very high pleasure, with bitter in it, too—as what pleasure is without it—to have a gracious message from one who has kept his singing robes unsullied—and I about to fling mine down in the mud of a 3/6 dinner to help some stupid woman across the intervals between the entrées.

But I am not so melancholy as all that, either: this is the morning after. I am sure you will believe me—because I trust you are not 'mistaken'—when I assure you that I set the greatest value on your good opinion, and am happy in the thought that my poetry should have given you pleasure—a master in the craft.

Will you tell me when, or if, you ever come to London, and we might meet, if it is your good pleasure, at my club.

Yours sincerely
John Davidson.

[1] (1844–1930), poet to whom John Lane had sent copies of D.'s work.

9
To Richard Le Gallienne
[1894] (extract)

20 Park Ridings,
Hornsey,
N.
Sunday

My dear Le Gallienne,

. . . After two ineffectual trials I have read *Religio Scriptoris*,[1] and am fully convinced that it is a book that ought to have been written and published, and certain to clear up the sky for many wavering souls, darkened souls, and certain to flutter the dovecots of the pseudo-Holy Ghost. It contains passages of the highest excellence and the freshest presentation of much advanced thought. Skal! But I mean to praise you highly when I say I don't like you in the pulpit. When you do your next 'Exodus from Houndsditch'[2] embody your opinions as in Narcissus.[3]

I am afraid the visit cannot be this year. Even had this week suited, when we came to face the matter, we saw much difficulty in leaving the house in the care of the servant who has been tried and found wanting in that particular: the boys are too much for her: we would on returning expect to find murder done or the house burned down or some worse catastrophe. As I said once before to you it will I am afraid be years before Mrs Davidson and I can pay and receive visits—and then we will be indifferent; as it is we are so unused to visiting that the thought of it makes us uncomfortable. Some day I may tell you how our

[1] The reference is to Le Gallienne's *The Religion of a Literary Man* (London, 1893).

[2] D. borrowed this phrase from Carlyle's *Journal* for 9 Feb. 1848, where it is used to suggest the end of the Judeo-Christian religion—quoted in J. A. Froude's *Thomas Carlyle: Life in London* (London, 1884). The district of Hounsditch was well known for its Jewish second-hand clothes dealers. D. used the phrase as the title of his apocalyptic 'A Ballad of the Exodus from Houndsditch' in *Ballads and Songs.*

[3] The reference is to Le Gallienne's autobiographical *The Book Bills of Narcissus* (London, 1891).

lives have been laid waste, and our moods and characters spoiled for society.

With kindest regards from us both to Mrs Le Gallienne and yourself.

I am
Yours ever
John Davidson.

10

To William Archer[1]

26 October 1894 (extract)

20 Park Ridings,
Hornsey. N.

Dear Mr Archer,

Accepting the idea of God the import is that God's sympathies are entirely with the nun: the Virgin on withdrawing tells her not only has she made herself one with Nature by employing her body, however blindly, for its appointed purpose, but also has made her self one with God while committing what she supposed to be deadly sin.

. . . But the author I imagine accepts no idea of God, and uses the most modern deity as he would Apollo or Odin. The whole idea of God the very word is obsolete: here is how he puts it in 'A Ballad of the Making of a Poet':

> 'If it be terrible into the hands
> Of the living God to fall, how much more dire
> To sicken face to face, like our sad age,
> Chained to an icy corpse of deity,
> Decked though it be and painted and embalmed!'

I look forward to meeting you with pleasure; but I won't be in town for a month. I have undertaken a certain piece of drudgery; I am far behind with it by reason of obstinate neuralgia, and must fasten myself down with beeswax till the end of November. In the beginning of December I shall see you I hope.

Yours sincerely
John Davidson.

[1] (1856–1924), London drama-critic and translator of Ibsen. He had written to D. after reading 'A Ballad of a Nun'.

11

To William Symingtm McCormick

11 April 1895 (extract)

20 Park Ridings,
Hornsey,
London N.

My dear McCormick,

. . . I am thirty-eight years old today, and am indulging myself in this gossip with you. I was never fitter in body and mind: my boys are well and are going down to a farm some six miles from Brighton in May where they will become more robust, and be taught something. My wife, whose relief from a very heavy burden, has not come too soon, is a little worn and tired, but she shall have a long rest now. Edinburgh[1] and my debts remain, but the former is not so bad as I am apt to imagine, and the latter I should be able to pay off without knowing it in a year or two.

Two months ago I gave up all my reviewing etc. . . . to do my own work, meaning to write poetry straight on for two years, and exhaust the lyric impulse that has come to me in my old age, thereafter at the age of forty to begin writing plays for the stage: 'The best laid plans'—can be improved upon and I shall be occupied for two or three months now in preparing a version of a French play for Forbes Robertson.[2] The commission was offered me, and I took it gladly; it will be a schooling for me.

You know Poe's[3] 'Haunted Palace'. The last two verses of it haunt me when I think of Porphyrogene[4] in Holloway:—

'But evil things in robes of sorrow,
  Assailed the monarch's high estate:
Ah let us mount!—for never morrow
  Shall dawn upon him desolate!
And round about his home the glory
  That blushed and bloomed
Is but a dim-remembered story
  Of the old time entombed.

And travellers now within the valley
  Through the red-litten windows, see

Vast forms, that move fantastically
  To a discordant melody;
While, like a ghastly rapid river,
  Through the pale door
A hideous throng rush out for ever
  And laugh—but smile no more.'

Porphyrogene, whom we admired both to his face and behind his back, who had in the greatest measure an unaccountable something which is genius.

Yours ever
John Davidson.

[1] At Edinburgh, D.'s brother Thomas was in poor mental health, and his mother and sister were suffering financial hardship.

[2] Johnston Forbes-Robertson (1853–1937), actor-manager at the Lyceum theatre, who played the male lead in D.'s adaptation of the French writer François Coppée's verse drama *Pour la courònne* (*For the Crown*) in 1896.

[3] Edgar Allan Poe (1804–49).

[4] Person born in the purple, ie a king or emperor, used here to refer to Oscar Wilde, who was taken to Holloway Prison following his conviction for homosexuality on 25 May 1895.

12

To William Symington McCormick

11 February 1897

Rayleigh House,
Shoreham,
Sussex.

My dear McCormick,

We had to get out of London at once. We naturally came here, to be near our boys. The town itself is the most doleful place we have ever lived in, and the first effect of it was to deepen the misery and hypochondria that drove us out of London. I think we are going to get well again, however. We shall be here for a year; at any rate until the end of Autumn. I hope to find out if I can really write a stage-play of my own.

My sister[1] has been staying with us since we came here. My wife and she get on very well.

There is no news: there cannot be any until this monstrous depression leaves us quite.

Yours ever
John Davidson.

[1] Euphemia (Effie) Davidson (1855–1935), who stayed with them for a while after her mother's death in Sept. 1896.

13
To William Symington McCormick
17 January 1899 (extract)

St. Winifred's,
Fairmile Avenue,
Streatham, S.W.[1]

My dear Mac,

For the first time in a year and a half we are able to breathe freely in this household.[2] The boys have gone to a good school, and have ceased to beleaguer our minds. That was really the terrible thing: two creatures, of ten and twelve now, dependent on us for everything, education, amusement, and we ignorant all the time where the bread and butter was to come from: the stupefaction and misery of this it is impossible to present except dramatically and it must be done sometime or other. Consider it: with my knowledge and experience of schools, it would have been criminal in me to send them to a cheap promiscuous school: the attempt to teach them—such a hateful relation between a father and his children: and Maggie thinking it, feeling it, knowing it: hers was by far the hardest burden. Without ample means to provide for them, men and women of any intelligence should not bring intelligent beings into the world; and if a man has any work of his own to do—I do not mean making money, or conquering an empire and [founding] a family—but if there is laid on him the necessity to [absorb] the world, and transmute it into words or sound or colour, he should have no children at all, at least until such time as the nature and necessities of this kind of man are recognised, and the responsibility of paternity is laid on the shoulders only of those who love it and wear it lightly. But this borders perilously on an inverted sentimentality.

I prepared the boys for school by taking them to Barnum and Baileys[3] where these extraordinary miscreants are to be seen—the dwarf, the giant, the brainless creature, the inarticulate wild man, the jointed twins—Sir, they haunt me still, and the meaning and interpretation of them I shall find out.

I further prepared the boys for school by taking them to the

Pantomime at Peckam which is the nearest to us. Here Marie Lloyd[4] is Dick Whittington, the genius of vulgarity, the artist in the jejune, in the phosphore and sordid, in blunt lechery—artist to her finger tips. She and Mrs Campbell[5] are the most interesting women on the stage I think. Both my little wretches understood these things, but are as harmless as doves. Have you read Henry James's 'Turn of the Screw'? To his old-maidish mind what he presents is to him very terrible, but it is the history of all children: that is how the knowledge of good and evil comes to them, only there is no foolish clairvoyante to kill them as a rule . . .

Yours ever
John Davidson.

[1] D. moved to Streatham in the autumn of 1898.
[2] He had received the first £150 of a grant of £250 from the Royal Literary Fund.
[3] The world-famous circus.
[4] (1870–1922), music-hall idol.
[5] Mrs Patrick Campbell (1865–1940); she and D. became friends when she played the female lead, as the slave-girl Militza, in D.'s adaptation of Coppée's *For the Crown* in 1896.

14
To John Lane
[copy of letter, March 1900][1]

My dear Lane,

When you told me some days ago that a pension for me was not beyond the bounds of possibility I began again to hope that I may yet be able to do something of what I long ago devised.

It was as an art always and not as a livelihood that I wished to follow literature; and during twelve years in Scotland with intercalary periods of starvation, quite helpful and healthy when a man is simple, I managed to make a wage in some capacity or other, and in my best hours wrote poetry, which is the only way to study poetry.

After marriage, however, I found that manner of existence impossible, and came to London to attempt to live by literature—the alternative in my case to giving it up entirely. I brought with me five dramatic poems, a volume of miscellaneous verse, and two volumes of stories, the latter being my first attempts to write for money. They were all commercial failures, but they gave me a certain standing.

My first two years in London I left poetry alone, having to take whatever work offered, if I could do it at all. But I could not make an income. In despair I returned to poetry, and my writings now began to attract some attention. For two years I seemed to be a successful author, but that was quite fortuitous, the accidents being the factitious vogue of a single poem,[2] and the admirable acting of Forbes Robertson and Mrs Campbell in a version of a play prepared by me.[3]

In the ten years since I left Scotland, besides translations, adaptations, reviewing, devilling etc., I have written two novels, two dramas, and five volumes of poetry. I am now forty-three; my health is shaken; and I cannot continue the struggle (I cannot; indeed, I cannot, under the old condition.) My boys whose health is also a constant source of anxiety—are thirteen and eleven. My wife, who has been more than a fortune, begins to wonder if the shadow will ever be lifted. I am paralysed by this:—although it is commonly acknowledged that I rank as a poet among the foremost of my time, there is no market for my poetry, and I can't now write anything else: for only in these forms can I get said what must be said.

I may count on another 10 years of life. If I could give my time unreservedly to my own things, I might make something of it yet: indeed I have it all to do; what I have written is only the porch and first day of a world I hoped to make. You will know better than I whether or not I should have written this, and will do what is wise with it.

Yours

[1] Written at Lane's request, when Lane was seeking to secure a state pension for D. D. was eventually awarded a Civil List pension of £100 a year in 1906. The facts of D.'s career outlined in this letter were well known to Lane.

[2] 'A Ballad of a Nun', first published in the *Yellow Book* in Oct. 1894. (Poem 19 in the present vol.)

[3] *For the Crown*, which ran from 27 Feb. to 30 May 1896 at the Lyceum theatre.

15
To William Archer
15 June 1901

Blairlogie,
Stirling, N.B.

My dear Archer,

You see I am out of humanity's reach.

Many thanks for your letter; but you put me in a great difficulty. There is or was a story of a German composer (told of Mendelssohn, I believe: I wish it had been a bigger man) who on being asked what a piece meant, played it on the piano, and said 'It means that'. The poet is in greater difficulty than the musician, because the musician had another medium of expression in spoken language; I unfortunately can't make music, or I would translate the 'Vivisector'[1] into a groaning, crashing overture to all opera.

I have no idea where to begin or what to say as you state only a general difficulty. My notion of the Vivisector is an imaginative one although I had in mind such Titans as Magendie, Bernard, Mantegazza.[2] I do not concern myself with the ordinary Vivisector who cuts up a dog or two in an underground room in a College because he believes it to be the thing to do just as the country curate will go to the *foyer* of the Empire when he visits London, because he thinks he is 'seeing life'; but the passionate, obsessed giant, hating religion, despising the 'humanities', searching into the secrets of Nature in his bloody way with the patience, delight, and self-torture of the artist, until the commonplace of the philosopher, that pain is normal and pleasure little more than an accident, flashes upon him with overwhelming meaning, and the whole Universe which he identifies with Matter becomes to him a reservoir of pain—an immense blind, dumb, unconscious artist, seeking for self-knowledge and expression at the cost of any agony. The poem is artistic, i.e. it is a statement of the Vivisector (the spin of a penny determined whether I should call the poems statements or testaments) not a condemnation or a criticism of him, but a dramatic account of him without any intention on the author's part to persuade the world for or against.—But all this may be beside the mark. If you were to ask me a question I would try to answer it.

Yours sincerely
John Davidson.

[1] *The Testament of a Vivisector* (1901).

[2] François Magendie (1783–1855), French physiologist who studied the spinal cord; Claude Bernard (1813–78), his pupil, whose physiological theories influenced Zola and the French naturalists; Paolo Mantegazza (1831–1900), Italian physiognomist and anthropologist.

16
To William Archer
29 November 1905 (extract)

9 Fairmile Avenue,
Steatham, S.W.

My dear Archer,

I am a brute for looking gift-horses in the mouth; but your reviews do tempt me.[1]

I am afflicted by your criticism of my form. The lines quoted for condemnation seem to me admirable: I use blank verse newly as Wagner did music. If you take a chromatic score of Wagner's and attempt to play it in common time in the key you will have a terrifying result. You can't sing-song my blank verse. But if you will do me the great kindness some day to take me through the passage you condemn I shall be very much your debtor.

Sincerely yours
John Davidson.

[1] Archer had criticized D.'s blank-verse drama *The Theatrocrat* in the *Daily Chronicle*, 27 Nov. 1905, 3. D. replied in two letters to the editor—'Theatrocratic', 28 Nov. 1905, 3; and 'At the Judgement-Seat', 20 Dec. 1905, 3.

17

To Max Beerbohm[1]

[8 April 1906]

9, Fairmile Avenue,
Streatham, S.W.
Sunday.

My dear Max,

I hope you are not going to Monte Carlo at Easter; because on Easter Monday if you are at liberty you can undertake the ineluctible adventure to which you are bound with me, the adventure of the Crystal Palace.[2] I shall show you this building without comeliness or colour, without life, without growth, without decay, and the gigantic featureless thing called mob, wandering aimlessly in masses and eddies, and if it rains for an hour or two, as I hope it may, you will find the place like a beach in Hades where souls are ground up together by an unseen sea, and Voltaire (Houdon's[3] statue) sitting grinning admist it, and Cellini's[4] Perseus, and Angelo's[5] Moses like the lost gods in Nifelheim.[6] I shall show you this as Virgil showed Dante terrible things; and our Paradiso shall be a seat at a window overlooking Surrey and a bottle of claret. It means a whole day. Let me know if Easter Monday will suit, and I shall send you your itinerary.

Yours ever
John Davidson.

[1] (1872–1956), author and cartoonist. He and D. became close friends in the 1890s.

[2] D. had already described the Crystal Palace in 'Automatic Augury and the Crystal Palace', *Glasgow Herald*, 18 Mar. 1905, 9. His poem 'The Crystal Palace' (36 in the present vol.) was written after his visit there with Beerbohm.

[3] Jean Antoine Houdon (1767–1855), French sculptor.

[4] Benvenuto Cellini (1500–71), Renaissance sculptor.

[5] Michael Angelo (1475–1564); his Moses is among his most famous sculptures.

[6] Cold region of perpetual night (Scandinavian mythology).

18
To Max Beerbohm
[16 April 1906] (extract)

9, Fairmile Avenue,
Streatham, S.W.
Easter Monday

My dear Max,

The tryst is made for Whitmonday. I shall write you a week before. A theatrical audience is a mob, so is a church audience, or a concert audience: each of these is *a* mob; but it has a mind, it is occupied with something, has a special purpose in assembling. But the crowd in the Crystal Palace on a bank holiday is not *a* mob; it is Mob, aimless, featureless, enormous, like the great Boyg.[1] It is four years since I encountered it. I am most curious to see if it can be encountered in company: probably, with you, it will cease to be Mob: probably it will be more Mob than ever.

I spent a day in Canterbury once. Had no such historical revelation vousafed me in the suicide of Thomas à Becket: felt only a dull interest in the Black Prince, and the Huguenot Chapel; and understood why Marlowe[2] wanted to get out of Christendom . . .

Yours ever,
John Davidson.

[1] A troll who has neither shape nor form, in Henrik Ibsen's play *Peer Gynt*.

[2] Christopher Marlowe (1564–93), Elizabethan playwright, who is said to have propagated atheistical opinions.

19
To Grant Richards[1]
20 February 1908

6, Coulson's Terrace,
Penzance.[2]

My dear Richards,

It means dismay and despondence from prolonged insomnia such as I have not had for several years;[3] and this hideous enfeeblement of asthma: these things set out a blank wall before me, and I require such great visions to be in health: indeed I now require to write blank verse daily if I am not to die: it is physiological: one could die of a constipated brain as well as otherwise. I begin to be well again, and to think of ten years instead of one or two in which to be and do greatly. Nevertheless there are things I cannot write of. I shall tell you when I see you. I hope to begin again the third part of 'God and Mammon'[4] as soon as we start printing the second and to have the third finished for Xmas at latest.

Disengage the 'Testaments' if you possibly can, the others can wait until they get into Madgwick's hands—if that is the name of the longshoreman who picks up unconsidered trifles in remainders.[5]

I wrote Filson Young[6] this morning, whom I am going to visit

[1] (1872–1948), publisher of D.'s works from 1901. He and D. became friends in 1894, when Richards was working as an assistant on C. K. Stead's *Review of Reviews.*

[2] D. moved to Penzance in 1907 to live cheaply and regain his health.

[3] Richards may have been alarmed by a cryptic comment in a business letter from D. on 17 Feb. 1908. D. had written: 'I have had a very distinct notice that I have hardly a year or two to live now.'

[4] The third part of *God and Mammon* was never written.

[5] Richards had gone bankrupt in 1904, and the stock of D.'s work had fallen into the hands of the receivers. Richards had started up in business again in 1905, using his wife's name, E. Grant Richards. Madgewick, Houlton and Co., Ltd., a firm of binders, owned the copyright of D.'s early books published by Ward & Downey.

[6] (1876–1938), author, journalist, and reader for Richards; he and D. became friends in 1905.

as soon as the weather suits, and asked him if you were ill: but I conclude you have unseated the influenza.

Kindest regards to Mrs Richards.

Yours ever
John Davidson.

20
To Max Beerbohm
20 April 1908 (extract)

6, Coulson's Terrace,
Penzance.

My dear Max,

. . . I came here a year ago to get well and to live on my pension. Should you ever require to get well, don't come to Penzance. Should you ever have a pension of £100 a year don't try to live on it[1]. This is wisdom. I have done neither, and abandon both attempts. The universe remains; and it is always necessary to be great.

Cornwall is a delusion of the guide-books and the interested railway. At Paddington Station 'Cornish Riviera Express' in large gilt letters on the best-equipped train in England might betray the wariest. A low-lying land of unworked tin mines, four hundred of them, grey, ghastly scabby ruins, inhabited by a lazy, lying, Wesleyan shoal of pilchards and congregation of choughs, there is nothing great about it, except the Atlantic, which is not Cornish alone. I want something great on the land—a mountain or a city. It is the greatness of London which is the profound subconscious satisfaction of living in it. Here, in Penzance, the wallflower blooms in the back-kitchen walls in March, arum-lilies grow like weeds, and flowering geraniums climb the houses like virginia-creepers; but all that is only novelty and one season exhausts it: only primeval, everlasting things are interesting, and these frequent the flanks of mountains and the streets of cities. Happily I know mountains and cities, and Cornwall doesn't matter. When the sun shines the sky is wonderful and so is Mount's Bay.

Yours ever,
John Davidson.

[1] D. had been awarded a Civil List Pension of £100 p.a. in 1906.

Index to First Lines

Index to Prose